MW00795341

"Doug Munton knows how to
Munton loves God's people. I've
Immersed, Doug combines these two traits to effectively call us closer
to God. Forty days of devotions—what a treasure. They combine
Doug's expertise with his humor and piercing discernment. He knows
what needs to be said and knows how to say it effectively. Prepare
yourself to draw closer to the Holy One."

JOHN MARSHALL, PASTOR
SECOND BAPTIST CHURCH, SPRINGFIELD, MO

"Doug Munton's 40-day devotional will guide you into a deeper walk
with Jesus Christ. As in the story he tells of jumping off the high diving
board into a swimming pool—it is not enough to get into the water;
we need to go deeper. And that is true. We need to go deeper with
Jesus Christ."

ELMER TOWNS, CO-FOUNDER
LIBERTY UNIVERSITY, LYNCHBURG, VA

"This is the best tool I have ever seen to unite a church during a forty-
day season. I wish I had this book years ago. Your church will change
if you use *Immersed*. And I mean, change in large and meaningful
ways. Go deep for forty days, and watch what God does!"

JOHN AVANT, SENIOR PASTOR
FIRST BAPTIST CHURCH OF CONCORD, TN
AUTHOR, *IF GOD WERE REAL* AND *AUTHENTIC POWER*

"Doug Munton takes you through the steps of diving deeper into your
faith and equips you with practical application. I recommend this
book as excellent reading for everyone, in all stages of their spiritual
walk. It is one that you will read many times."

DAVID UTH, SENIOR PASTOR
FIRST BAPTIST CHURCH, ORLANDO, FL

"One of the most important things a believer can do is to spend time daily with Jesus. Pastor Doug, in his new book, *Immersed*, provides a pathway to further our relationship with Jesus and our understanding of God's word. On this 40-day journey, you will be challenged and inspired to plunge joyously deeper into faith."

GREGG MATTE, SENIOR PASTOR
HOUSTON'S FIRST BAPTIST CHURCH, HOUSTON, TX

"For any Christian, at whatever stage of your faith journey, I encourage you to *come on in* and utilize this new devotional resource because the *water is fine*!

DR. PRESTON NIX, PROFESSOR AND DIRECTOR
LEAVELL CENTER FOR EVANGELISM AND CHURCH HEALTH
NEW ORLEANS BAPTIST THEOLOGICAL SEMINAR

"Allow Doug Munton to lead you on a journey to a place of intimacy and deeper faith in Christ in this magnificent work, *Immersed: 40 Days to a Deeper Faith*. This is a must-read for anyone interested in taking their relationship with God to the next level!"

AARON BROYLES, ENTREPRENEUR
AUTHOR OF *DO GREAT THINGS*

IMMERSED

DOUG MUNTON

IMMERSED:

40 DAYS TO A DEEPER FAITH

Published by
Deep River Books
Sisters, Oregon
www.deepriverbooks.com

ISBN-13:9781937756987
ISBN-10:193775698X

Library of Congress: 2013943346

Printed in the USA

Cover design by David Litwin, Purefusion Media

Dedication

This book is dedicated to two great heroes who died recently. My father, Eldon Munton, lived out his faith before me all of my life. He was kind and wise and godly, and that was evident to all who knew him. His goodness and commitment to the Lord Jesus are examples I want to follow. He lived well and died well, and I miss him.

Dr. Roy Fish was my professor and friend. I appreciated him as a professor, admired him as a preacher, and respected him as a man of God. We became prayer partners and friends in these last years and I will miss his insight, passion, and kindness.

Foreword

There are Christians who play in the waters of Christianity, and then there are those who learn to plunge into the deeper waters with the Lord as they daily and intimately spend time with him in his Word. Doug Munton, a longtime friend, has given us a rare gift. In this, we have a 40-day, easy-to-follow guide that will assist and encourage us to join the Old Testament prophet Ezekiel (Ezekiel 47) as we leave the ankle-deep water of Christianity and follow Jesus into the fathomless depths of his love. We will learn to enjoy the thrill of being "in over our head" with Christ and savor every minute of it!

This well-crafted course will inspire and strengthen you as you bathe in the eternal truths of three of the Bible's most encouraging books— John, Acts, and Proverbs. In John, you will learn more about who Jesus is, as you plunge into the waters with the disciple referred to as "the one Jesus loved." In Proverbs, you will immerse yourself in the amazing, practical wisdom given by King Solomon, one of the wisest men ever to live. You will also enjoy the refreshing living water of the Holy Spirit as you bask in the verses of my favorite book of the Bible—Acts.

Doug is uniquely qualified to write concerning this subject. He has been a believer for over forty years. He is also a veteran pastor who has helped shepherd God's flock for several decades. Through preaching and teaching God's Word, discipling new believers in the words and ways of Jesus, and providing a steady and consistent Christlike example, Doug has consistently demonstrated to others exactly what it means to plunge deeply into a vibrant relationship with the living God. He has walked intimately with Christ while being simultaneously engaged with the daily (even hourly) responsibilities of a husband, father, pastor, preacher, denominational servant, and friend.

The words you are about to read are not from some novice, armchair philosopher. Doug does NOT pontificate from an idealistic ivory tower concerning matters about which he knows little or nothing. Rather, Doug Munton is a genuine expert who has already walked faithfully down the road of life with Jesus while concurrently leading a busy and full life. He knows what he is talking about, because he has "been there and done that." The longer you live, the more you realize that a mentor like that is the only kind worth following.

In a day when so many are content with shallow Christianity, Doug Munton's guide, *Immersed: 40 Days to a Deeper Faith*, is just what our churches need. He prudently shows us how to move on from the elementary things of Christianity, so we can experience the deeper spiritual realm we have long desired. As a fellow spiritual swimmer, I assure you: Once you dive into these life-changing waters and experience the ecstasy of being *Immersed* in a deeper and daily walk with God in His Word, you will never go back to the shallow end again!

Enjoy the plunge!

3 John 2

Steve Gaines, PhD, Senior Pastor
Bellevue Baptist Church
Memphis, Tennessee

Contents

Introduction

> Though by this time you ought to be teachers, you need some-
> one to teach you again the basic principles of God's revelation.
> You need milk, not solid food.
>
> HEBREWS 5:12

I still remember my first time jumping off the high dive.

In the summertime I spent a lot of afternoons at the community pool in my small town. Most of my time was spent in the shallow end, splashing and playing with my brothers and friends. I watched other kids jumping off the diving boards at the deep end of the pool. It seemed fun and exciting, but too scary for me.

As the summer progressed, I thought more and more about what it would be like to overcome my fears and worries and plunge into the deep, blue water of the deep end. I even walked by that area of the pool a few times to calculate the possibilities. The deep water was so inviting, yet I was so frightened to plunge in.

Finally, I could take it no longer. I had to abandon the shallow end and experience the depth of the other side. I had to try something more than the kids' side of the pool. I made my way to the ladder that ascended to the diving board.

I'm sure it wouldn't seem so big now, but at the time it seemed to be monstrously tall. As I waited for an older boy to dive in, a line began to form behind me. There was no turning back now without the pungent odor of humiliation clinging to me ferociously throughout the next school year.

The older boy completed his dive—something fancy that ended in a cascade of water droplets. It was time. I began to climb the steel rungs of the ladder one by one. Each rung took me higher and brought greater fear and anxiety. Finally, I reached the rough surface of the diving board. I slowly walked toward the end and felt it bend and sway beneath my feet.

There would be no spectacular dive for me. I wasn't doing any back flips or twists—just a simple step off and a feet-first plunge. But that step was a big one. Finally, with a mixture of terror and exhilaration, I stepped off and plunged deeper than I had ever been.

The pool was never the same after that. I was no longer limited to the one side populated by moms and their children. Plunging into the cold, clear water became a regular part of my summer, and I was officially a swimmer.

Many of us live our spiritual lives in the shallow end when God wants us to plunge deeper into faith. He wants us to learn and stretch and grow. Yet we remain in the shallow end, never knowing the exhilaration of deepened discipleship. Without plunging in, we never learn the excitement of following Christ. Without plunging in, we never learn the astonishing joy of living the life God made us to enjoy.

There are two areas I want to ask you to commit to specifically as you begin this 40-day journey. The first area is salvation. I urge you—if you haven't already done this—to repent of your sins and place your faith in Jesus Christ. Admit that you have sinned against Him and that this sin separates you from Him. Trust that Jesus died on the cross to pay for your sins and that He rose from the dead to conquer the power of sin over you. Place your faith in the Lord Jesus and be saved.

Salvation is just the beginning of your spiritual life. When you repent of your sins and place your faith in Christ who died for you, you experience a new beginning. This salvation is the starting place and it is great and eternal. Salvation, however, is not the ending point of your spiritual life; it is the beginning. God wants you to grow in discipleship.

The second area I ask you to commit to is growing in discipleship. Discipleship is plunging deeper into faith. It involves a strengthening of your understanding of the Lord and your obedience to His purposes and plans. Discipleship is going beyond the elementary principles of God's Word and being immersed in the whole truth. God made you to go deeper, to learn more, and to apply the lessons He teaches you.

This is a 40-day journey to a deeper faith. It will be a gentle prod toward deepening your spiritual understanding and following the Lord in every area of your life.

For the next 40 days I want to ask the following of you:

- Read the devotional for that day. Rather than read the whole book at one setting, read one devotional each day for the next 40 days. It will begin a healthy pattern for discipleship.

- Read two chapters in the Bible each day. You will find them under the "Today's Bible Reading" section at the end of each day. You will read three books of the Bible in their entirety during these 40 days—John, Proverbs, and Acts. I recommend that you underline verses in your Bible each day that are especially helpful to you or ones you want to remember.

- Think through the "Questions to Consider" section for each day. These are questions that are designed to get you to think through the personal application of each devotional.

While these 40 days can be done alone, they are best completed when discussed with a small group each week. Consider doing this devotional in connection with a small group or Sunday school class or alongside some friends. We are designed by God for connection with others, and a group setting will prove to be a great blessing for this study.

Finally, ask God to use these next 40 days in a special way. I'm praying that God will get your full attention and that you will begin to learn and grow and deepen your faith in an awesome way these next days.

Now, let's plunge in!

Chapter One

SOAKING IT ALL UP: KNOWING AND FOLLOWING GOD'S WORD

⁓⌇⌇⁓

A vital part of plunging deeper into faith is to soak up all God has for us to know and to do. Like a dry sponge soaks up water, we are made to soak up God's Word. We will see the value of knowing and following God's Word this week. Ask God to give you a mind that is seeking and a heart that is hungry. Soak up all God has for you each day.

Getting an Education

My people are destroyed for lack of knowledge.

HOSEA 4:6

You've got a lot to learn.

When you were in kindergarten, you might have thought you knew almost everything. And then you discovered complex math and chemistry and English novels and Spanish. There was a lot more to learn than you realized.

God has so much for you to learn. He wants you to know about His character and your nature, ethical expectations, and behavioral changes. He wants you to learn from biblical history and be inspired by poetic worship, to know your hidden abilities and your subtle dangers. You've got a lot to learn.

One of the most important ways to plunge deeper into faith is to learn God's Word, and through that, to learn of His plan for your life. God gave you the great gift of the Bible as a means of learning what it means to be a fully committed disciple of Jesus.

I visited my grandmother during my seminary days. Grandma Miller taught an older women's Sunday school class in her church and she took it seriously. So, she began to pepper her young seminary grandson with Bible questions and theological issues.

Now, there were some things I knew that my grandmother didn't. I had taken Greek and Hebrew and systematic theology classes. But it soon became apparent to me that my grandmother knew the Bible in a way that I didn't. While I had taken classes, she had spent a lifetime reading the Bible. She knew the Bible in a more intimate way than I did. Over the years, she had been immersed in personal Bible reading and study.

I determined that day that I wanted to know the Bible like that. I wanted to know it the way my grandmother knew it. And I began a more serious approach to reading the Bible day by day.

Since that time I have made it my practice to read the Bible through at least once every year. That was a long time ago now and I've read the Bible through many, many times. From that, I have some observations.

First, it takes some time to begin to put things together. How does the Old Testament relate to the New Testament? Who is this biblical character again? Haven't I seen his name before? How does this idea in one Bible book relate to that idea in another Bible book? What is the full nature of the gospel message? All of these things take some time to understand and connect.

━∿ ∼━

Every great task is made up of a series of smaller tasks.

━∿ ∼━

I think you need to read the Bible through six or seven times before things really begin to click. By your tenth or twelfth time through the Bible, some of those questions begin to gain clarity and you start to put the story of the Bible together in a more cohesive way.

Second, learning the Bible is not a one-day—or one-year—task. It requires some consistency over a long period of time. Many start with great intentions only to be defeated by the enormity of the task. Every great task is made up of a series of smaller tasks. You won't finish the Bible today, but you can read the first two chapters of the book of John today.

Begin the healthy practice of reading some each day. Like exercise, Bible reading needs a pretty regular regimen. (I encourage people in our church to read the Bible every day, but say that five out of seven days is a pretty healthy pattern for exercise and for Bible reading.) After finishing these 40 days of *Immersed* and the Bible reading that goes with it each day, set a goal of reading the 260 chapters of the New Testament this year. That is very doable and well worth the effort.

Third, recognize that some days will be better than others. Some books are easier to read. Some Bible stories match where you are in life more than others. Some days you feel better than others. Let's face it, some days you are grumpy or tired or whiny or lazy.

Going deeper in faith involves doing the right things even when you may not feel like it or when it is difficult. I've even noticed that some of my best days of learning from the Bible began when I didn't really feel like starting.

Pick up a Bible and let's get started. We've got a lot to learn.

⁓⌇⌇⁓

DAY ONE: SOAKING IT ALL UP

Verse to Remember: Hosea 4:6: "My people are destroyed for lack of knowledge."

Questions to Consider: Knowing that I need the healthy practice of reading my Bible regularly, what goal can I set for my personal Bible reading? After reading two chapters a day for the 40 days of *Immersed*, what goal might I set? Five of seven days each week? Reading the 260 chapters of the New Testament through in six months (five days per week, two chapters per day)?

Today's Bible Reading: John 1–2.

Turn the Light On

Your word is a lamp for my feet and a light on my path.

Psalm 119:105

Walking in the dark is a good way to stub your toe.

It is rather obvious that if you can't see where you're going, you are going to have some problems. And the path of life can be pretty dark. God gives us the Bible so we can see the right direction and avoid the dangers and pitfalls of life in a fallen world.

Plunging deeper in faith can't happen without knowing where to swim. Many are swimming through life aimlessly, not sure where to turn or what to do. They paddle frantically but with little progress, not knowing their goal or purpose.

I was deep in the forest, hunting on some unfamiliar property. I had followed a particular path into the tree stand without a problem during the light of day. Now it was dark and I was without a flashlight. Not a smart move.

As I headed back to the farmhouse where my car was parked, it didn't take long for me to lose track of the leaf-covered path. Soon I was wandering aimlessly in the woods. Roots tripped my steps, vines caught my boots, and fallen trees blocked my path. I couldn't tell north from south or east from west. Now tell me: Why did I go out there without a flashlight?

And then I saw it. There in the distance was a light. The faint glimmer of the light from the farmhouse I was seeking twinkled in the distance. I followed the light and made it back home.

God's purpose and plan for our life is much like a path. But there is so much we cannot see. We can't see what the future holds and we can easily miss the tripping roots and sunken holes along the way. But God gives us His Word to bring clarity to the direction we are to take.

God's Word illuminates the truth about our circumstances and our opportunities. It is given to us to provide clarity to our world's fuzzy morality and confused standards. Through the Bible we are able to see the dangers of temptation and the opportunities of ministry.

There are three good reasons (among many) why I need to turn on the light of God's Word in my life: for discernment, for difficulties, and for the destination.

⟨⟨⟨∼∼⟩⟩⟩

God's Word brings clarity to our path.

⟨⟨⟨∼∼⟩⟩⟩

Discerning disciples know that God's way is right and good and best. But there are many other paths we can follow instead of God's path. Some are on a wrong path right now without even realizing it. They might lack the discernment to know the difference between right and wrong paths. "Aren't all paths leading to the same place?" they ask. Would you ask that if you were driving somewhere?

Discernment means that we can recognize right from wrong, good from bad—even good from great. God gives His Word so we can avoid all the wrong directions of life and follow His best for our lives.

There are some difficulties on the path God calls us to follow. The world's way is often the easy way and God's way is often difficult. The Bible teaches us about the awesome, but difficult, path of discipleship.

The way of the disciple is often uphill and narrow and long. But it is also right and good and best. God encourages us through His Word to persevere and to triumph. He helps us overcome our grief, loneliness, past failures, and broken relationships.

One of the great benefits of the light of God's Word is that it points us toward our destination. It points us toward eternal life and the things that will matter forever. It points us toward an abundant life where we find meaning and purpose and fulfillment during the journey.

God's plan for your life is the only place you can find the deep-down joy and fulfillment your heart is searching for. And the details and principles of finding God's plan are found in His Word to us. No other path can bring the blessings God wants you to enjoy. Every path leads some-where. Only God's path leads you to the place of ultimate peace and blessing. Only God's Word can illuminate your way to that destination.

Some of you are like I was in the woods. You're wandering around in the dark, unsure of where to go or what to do. You need some light. You need to begin to learn and understand and comprehend the Bible in a way that you haven't to this point.

Or maybe you feel like you're doing just fine right now. Your path seems pretty clear. But prepare and read now, knowing that storm clouds will darken the sky at some point in your journey.

Every journey begins with a step. Open God's Word. Begin to dis-cover the direction He has for you. And follow the light He gives to your path.

—∿∿—

DAY TWO: SOAKING IT ALL UP

POINTS TO PONDER

Verse to Remember: Psalm 119:105: "Your word is a lamp for my feet and a light on my path."

Questions to Consider: What do I know God wants me to do right now that I'm not currently doing? What do I know God wants me to stop? In what area of my life do I most need the light of God's Word?

Today's Bible Reading: John 3–4.

A Guide for the Journey

When the Spirit of truth comes, He will guide you into all the truth.

JOHN 16:13

The Guide knows the way.

Trying to describe the nature of God reminds one of the essay question a college professor is said to have given on a test. It said: "Describe the universe. Give three examples." Not easily done.

The Bible tells us about our triune God: He is one God with three ways of being. Though the word "trinity" is not found in the Bible, the concept of the trinity certainly is. God is—and always has been and always will be—one God in three persons.

God the Holy Spirit, like God the Father and God the Son, is often spoken of in the Bible. And the Bible tells us that He has the purpose of guiding us in our understanding of the truth.

Jesus describes the Holy Spirit in our focal passage as "the Spirit of truth" who guides us into all the truth. In other words, God's Spirit lives in the believer, serving as the Guide on his or her journey into knowing and understanding the truth.

—~∿∽~—

You don't face the task of understanding God's will on your own.

—~∿∽~—

You don't face the task of understanding God's will on your own. Our Guide helps us to understand God's Word. He convicts us when we do wrong. He encourages us to follow the path of truth carefully.

A group of us visited Israel some years ago. None of us had been there before, but we were excited to learn about the land of the Bible and to see where Jesus walked. I suppose we might have taken off on

DOUG MUNTON

our own and tried to figure out where we were and where to go. But thankfully, we had guides to help us.

Our guides knew what they were doing. We had a seminary professor who had been to Israel many times and related the Bible stories to the geography we travelled. There was an Israeli who knew the land from birth and who had insights into the culture and conditions of the land. They were invaluable to our experience.

The Holy Spirit is our Guide. He is invaluable to us as we try to follow the path of deeper discipleship. His direction is critical to fully understanding the gospel. He guides in two important ways.

First, the Holy Spirit is our Guide in that He helps us to understand the Word. The Bible is big and complex. Our Guide is always pointing us to the truth of the word and illuminating it in our hearts. He urges us to study the Bible, and He enables our study to be productive.

Ask God for help in understanding His Word. Ask Him to help you know what it meant long ago and what it means to you today. God wants us to do our part—to read and study and memorize and think. But the Spirit of truth will help us understand and apply that truth.

It is not impossible to understand the Bible. It does take effort and it does take persistence. But, we have another means by which we gain understanding of God's Word. The Holy Spirit will help us in the important task of illuminating and applying the Word to our hearts.

The Holy Spirit is a Guide in another sense of the word. Not only does He help us understand God's Word, He also helps us follow God's way. He convicts us, the Bible says, about "sin, righteousness, and judgment" (John 16:8). He helps us know right from wrong and good from evil. He helps us find and follow the right path for our lives.

Imagine for a moment that you're hiking in a massive national park when you suddenly realize you're lost. You don't know which way to go or where to find help. Fortunately for you, a park ranger walks by. He sees you, speaks to you, and finds out about your situation. Well, the problem is solved. The ranger certainly knows the way out and can help you follow the right path.

This world has so many choices. Many of the paths lead somewhere other than God's best. How do we know the right way to go? How can we find the way? The Holy Spirit serves as our Guide. By pointing us to the Bible, and through conviction and encouragement, He leads us on the path that is God's will.

Our focal verse tells us the Holy Spirit will guide us "into all the truth." All the truth means God wants us to know the parts we like and the parts we don't. The Spirit leads us to the parts of the truth that are easy for us and the parts that are hard.

God wants us to know the whole truth. And because He does, He has sent us the Holy Spirit who will help us understand and will lead us on our journey.

〜〜〜

Day Three: Soaking It All Up

Points to Ponder

Verse to Remember: John 16:13: "When the Spirit of truth comes, He will guide you into all the truth."

Questions to Consider: How does knowing that the Holy Spirit guides us into all the truth help me in my personal Bible reading? Might the truth sometimes be uncomfortable or unpopular? In what ways? Can I trust God with every aspect of my life?

Today's Bible Reading: John 5–6.

Examining the Evidence

They welcomed the message with eagerness and examined
the Scriptures daily to see if these things were so.

Acts 17:11

Is it true?

We are invited to read the Bible for ourselves and to examine the evidence closely. We can read, think, question, and consider. We can compare and contrast. We can study and speculate. We have the great opportunity to read the Bible and consider the claims it makes.

I believe the Bible is true, that it is God's Word to us. I believe it has the power to change lives and relationships and eternal things. I have examined the evidence for myself and believe it to be God's word for our lives.

But you don't have to take my word for it. You can examine the evidence for yourself. You can read it and study it on your own.

The Bible tells us in Acts 17 of how Paul and Silas went to the synagogue in Beroea. We are told that they were more "open-minded" than those in other cities had been. We are told that "they welcomed the message with eagerness." That is, they were excited to hear the message of the gospel.

They listened carefully as they were told that God became a man in Jesus Christ, that Christ died for our sins, and that He rose from the dead. They heard that they were to repent of their sins and believe on Jesus and that they could be saved from the penalty of sin.

This was a message they welcomed for it was truly good news—if it was true. That one could be saved from the penalty of sin by the sacrifice of Jesus on the cross was something to be excited about—if it was true. Forgiveness was full and free in Christ, hope was given to sinful man, one could be washed as white as snow; these were awesome truths—if they were true.

Their questions concerned the truth.

DOUG MUNTON

And so the Beroeans did something remarkable. They examined the Scriptures daily. They studied to see if this gospel message matched the Scriptures. Did these teachings match the law and the prophets? Did the Old Testament contradict or correlate with the New Testament?

Verse 12 tells us the result. "Consequently, many of them believed." They examined carefully and they discovered the message to be real. God was not distant and far removed. He was aware of their sinful plight and provided a means of forgiveness.

They became convinced that the gospel message was true.

—⟋⟋⟍⟋⟍—

God wants us to study and think.

—⟋⟋⟍⟋⟍—

Detective shows and books have been popular for years. Detectives examine the evidence to find the guilty and exonerate the innocent. Forensic technology and DNA evidence have changed the nature of the work now. But one thing remains: a search for the truth.

God invites our inquiry. He wants us to study and think. No one has to put aside their intellect to come into the church doors or to open their Bibles. Truth can stand the questioning. In fact, truth invites the questioning, knowing that it can lead to a deep and genuine faith.

When I was in college, I came to an important moment of inquiry. I had some questions and even perhaps some doubts about the faith. A well-meaning friend suggested that it didn't matter. The Christian faith was the best way to live regardless of whether it was true or not. But I wasn't wired that way.

I came to a maxim: If the Bible isn't true, I wasn't going to live as though it was. But, the other side of that commitment followed. If the Bible is true, I wasn't going to live as though it wasn't.

I searched the evidence, considered the alternatives, read apologetics, and thought and prayed. I came to the unmistakable conclusion, like the Beroeans before me, that the Bible is true and the gospel is real. The more I studied the faith, the more convinced I became it was true.

I might not know all the answers to all the questions, but I became convinced that I could trust God's Word.

You can study and think and ask for yourself. You can stop at the Christian bookstore and read the many wonderful books on apologetics found there. I'm convinced that the more you learn, the more you'll find the Bible to be trustworthy. But you don't have to take my word for it. You can examine the Scriptures yourself.

The Bible can stand up to our questions. It is true and truth is unkillable. Study, read, and examine it for yourself.

DAY FOUR: EXAMINING THE EVIDENCE

Verse to Remember: Acts 17:11: "They welcomed the message with eagerness and examined the Scriptures daily to see if these things were so."

Questions to Consider: Do I believe the Bible is true? If I'm not sure, am I willing to examine the evidence? If the Bible is true, am I willing to live as though it is?

Today's Bible Reading: John 7–8.

The Heart of the Matter

I have treasured Your word in my heart so
that I may not sin against You.

PSALM 119:11

Your heart is critical.

David is described in the Bible as "a man after God's own heart." It doesn't mean that he was perfect, of course. The Bible clearly shows us the imperfections of people, David included. It means that he was passionate about his relationship with the Lord. He had a deep love for the things of God that sprang from deep within his very being.

There is an unbreakable connection between your treasure and your heart. Jesus said it like this, "For where your treasure is, there your heart will be also" (Matthew 6:21).

The things that really matter to you are the things that you focus on, think about, and contemplate. The psalmist tells us that he treasured and placed in his heart something of great value and importance. Deep in his heart was that which he most cherished. That thing of great value was God's Word.

A friend of mine told me about preaching on the back of a flatbed truck next to Red Square in Moscow some years ago. The communist government had just fallen and many people there were searching for meaning and purpose. My friend was put on the back of the truck, given a microphone, and told to preach to the walking masses through a translator.

If we tried that in America, we would be ignored or mocked. But people in Moscow, hungry for spiritual food, listened. Then, the organizers of the flatbed preaching tour caused unintentional pandemonium. They announced that Russian language Bibles would be given away.

My friend told me that the next moments were like being at a rock concert. The people crushed toward the truck to get a Bible. Every Bible was given out in moments and a mass of humanity cried for more. Many had never owned a Bible or read a word from it. But they longed to see it for themselves.

What a difference in America. We have easy access to the Bible. Many have copies of God's Word sitting in their bedrooms and on their coffee tables. But, often, that is about as close as it ever gets to our hearts.

What if we treasured it? What if we saw its great value and it became so important to us that our heart longed to know it?

⸻

We treasure God's Word because we treasure Him.

⸻

The psalmist gives us the reason for why he has so treasured God's Word. "...so that I may not sin against You." In other words, he deeply treasured the Word of God because he so deeply treasured his relationship with God.

One of the reasons God wants you to know His Word is because He wants you to avoid all the dangers and damage that comes to your life through sin. Sin always harms us; it always leaves us with hurt and pain and damage.

Sin does damage to us, but it also does damage to our most important relationship—our relationship with God. Sin separates us from God, which is why we need salvation and forgiveness. But sin also damages our fellowship with God even after salvation.

When my children were little I would give them some rules and some boundaries. Sometimes they would test the enforcement of those rules and the firmness of those boundaries. When they did wrong, it was damaging to our fellowship. They never stopped being my children, of course, but the fellowship and closeness we had was strained when they disobeyed. And that strain was not enjoyable for me or for them.

If you want a deeper and closer relationship with God, He will remind you of some rules and boundaries. He does that because He loves you and wants what is best for you, just like parents want the best for their children. But He also tells us that our fellowship with Him is affected by our willingness to avoid the sinfulness of disobedience.

If you want to dive deeper in faith, treasure God's Word in your heart. Know it in such a way that you will know what it teaches about sin, about right and wrong, and about good and bad. Out of that commitment will come a deepening in your relationship with the Lord and a strengthening of your faith.

God's Word gets to the heart of the matter. Let the matter of God's Word get to your heart.

―∽∾―

DAY FIVE: THE HEART OF THE MATTER

POINTS TO PONDER

Verse to Remember: Psalm 119:11: "I have treasured Your word in my heart so that I may not sin against You."

Questions to Consider: What do I think the psalmist means when he says that he has treasured God's Word in his heart? What might change if I begin to really treasure God's Word in my own heart? Is God's Word so valuable to me that I am willing to obey it? Is there an area of my life God wants me to correct right now?

Today's Bible Reading: John 9–10.

Reaching the Goal

Now the goal of our instruction is love from a pure heart,
a good conscience, and a sincere faith.

1 TIMOTHY 1:5

You have a goal to reach.

Having a goal can be very helpful. It can keep you on track and motivated. It can remind you of where you're going and why you do what you do. Athletes often have goals that motivate their training. Explorers have goals that guide their travels. Business leaders have goals that guide their decisions and their planning.

God has a goal for you and your Bible instruction. And it is more than that you are better at playing Bible Trivia or remembering the names of the disciples or the twelve tribes of Israel. It is more than that you can argue the finer points of theology better than the other person in your Bible study class. The goal is much more than that.

God wants you to know His Word so that you will love deeply and clearly.

At Christian weddings it is fairly common for 1 Corinthians 13 to be read. This beautiful chapter of the Bible tells us what genuine love is and what it isn't. It also tells us how important love really is. According to this passage, we are merely "a sounding gong or a clanging cymbal" if we know the languages of men and angels but don't have love (v. 1). We gain absolutely nothing if we give all our resources to feed the poor, but don't have love (v. 3).

God wants more from you than just some changes on the outside. God wants you to learn to love—to love Him and to love others. Your goal is more than keeping rules or knowing information. Your goal is to love the Lord and to love others just as the Lord loves you.

In my early days of Sunday school classes, we had envelopes that gave percentages totaling up to 100% for certain activities you performed. You received 10% for bringing your Bible, 10% if you invited someone

DOUG MUNTON

38

to class, and some other percentages if you studied your lesson in advance and engaged in other things you should be doing anyway. It was a simple way of reminding us of things we ought to do.

⟶∿⟋⟍∿⟵

Your goal is more than rules or information.

⟶∿⟋⟍∿⟵

But that system had a flaw. There was no percentage connected to love. There was no quantification given for loving God or others. It could gauge the outside responsibilities, but not the inner obligations. External behavior could be noted, but not the weightier goal of love.

God wants you to read and know His Word. But He has a goal beyond just marking off that you read two chapters today. He wants you to read it and know it so you will learn to love as He loves.

Our focal passage reminds us that this kind of love comes from "a pure heart, a good conscience, and a sincere faith." Love—the goal of our instruction—comes from within, not just from the external works we have performed.

The Lord calls us to "love from a pure heart." This gets to our motives. We might do the right things for the wrong reasons. For instance, we might be involved in a ministry—serving, helping, teaching, etc. These are all good things. But, we might do them for the wrong reasons—to gain recognition or so others will be obligated to help us, or so we can be in charge. The Lord wants us to do the right things for the proper reasons.

We are told to love from "a good conscience." You may not be able to please everyone else. If you've lived trying to pleasing everyone, you already know how impossible that is. Fortunately, you don't have to. You are to live to please your Lord. If you do your best to honor the Lord and obey His will, it really doesn't matter if you please anyone else. If you, in good conscience, have done your best and done it for the glory of God, that is the act of love the Lord desires.

The Bible tells us to love from "a sincere faith." Sincerity always matters to the Lord. You may fool others, but never the Lord. He is looking for more than the artificial love we see so often in our world: "I will love you if…" or "I will love you when…." Hypocrisy is repugnant to our Savior. He wants your love to be like His—real, genuine, sincere.

The goal of working through *Immersed* for these 40 days is to learn to love the Lord more completely and to love others more fully. He gives us His Word so that we will learn to love in the same way that He has loved us.

Read for the goal of love. Study for the goal of love. Keep that goal before you as you gain knowledge and understanding through your Bible reading, worship services, and Bible classes. Ask the Lord to teach you through His Word how to love Him and others more. Ask Him to help you love other people as He loves you.

Reach for the goal.

———

Day Six: Reaching the Goal

Points to Ponder

Verse to Remember: 1 Timothy 1:5: "Now the goal of our instruction is love from a pure heart, a good conscience, and a sincere faith."

Questions to Consider: How does the Lord love me and how does that help me to love others? Why is love so important? What is the danger of not understanding "the goal of our instruction"?

Today's Bible Reading: John 11–12.

Consistency Counts

You must speak what is consistent with sound teaching.

TITUS 2:1

Consistency counts.

It counts in families (does a husband want his wife to be faithful much of the time?), in business (do you want to purchase from people who are honest with you once in a while?), and restaurants ("don't worry, the food here is good once every three times we try it"). Consistency counts in many areas. But nowhere is consistency more important than in the knowing, obeying, and teaching of God's Word.

The book of Titus is a letter from Paul to Titus, Paul's "true child in our common faith" (Titus 1:4). Paul wants Titus to help the believers in Crete. He is to help them learn and live the truth and to overcome any incorrect teaching or misunderstanding they might have. Titus is to "set right what was left undone" (Titus 1:5) and help the believers in Crete to follow the sound teaching of God's Word.

The value of learning the concept of consistency is important for many reasons. But there are three especially important reasons for God's emphasis on consistent teaching.

First, God is consistent. God is truth and truth does not waver. He "is the same yesterday, today, and forever" (Hebrews 13:8). He is always consistent with Himself.

On occasion a news report might tell of someone who committed some heinous crime and then said, "God told me to do it." We can rightly say, "No, God didn't tell you to commit that sinful act." God is consistent with Himself and His holiness. You wrongly understood or listened to an imitator of God's voice. But God is consistent.

Second, God's Word is consistent. God's Word is true and consistent and non-contradictory. His Word tells us the truth and that applies forever.

Scoffers delight in pointing out supposed inconsistencies in the

Bible. I once read of a prominent personality who left any following of orthodox faith when she heard the teaching of the Bible that God is a jealous God. She reasoned that God could not be good if He was jealous. She misunderstood a relatively simple concept, I think.

─∿∾─

Know the truth, teach the truth, and live the truth.

─∿∾─

She failed to see that God is jealous in the sense that He wants us to worship only Him, the only true and living God. It is not that God is worried or fearful or uncertain or petty. It is a linguistic tool that teaches us a consistent truth: There is only one God, and all other worship is futile and folly.

The longer I study the Bible, the more I have come to understand its consistency and trustworthiness. There are things I have yet to fully understand, of course, but I see more clearly the trustworthy nature of God's Word the more I have learned. The supposed inconsistencies have more to do with our own misunderstanding of figures of speech and cultural meanings and limited insight. God calls us to follow sound teaching because His Word is just that—sound.

Third, God's people are to follow the consistency of His teaching. We are to study and learn in such a way that we can clearly and accurately teach others the truth of God. We are to so immerse ourselves in the Word that we know the truth, teach the truth, and live the truth.

God wants us to learn His truth clearly so we can clearly teach His truth to others. As we teach our Bible studies, our Vacation Bible School classes, our children and grandchildren, the Lord wants us to teach carefully and clearly and consistently.

Many believers know only bits and pieces of God's Word. They have yet to grasp the full picture of God's redemptive work and the cohesive nature of God's remarkable Word. Paul is saying to Titus what he certainly wants us to know today, "Learn and study and comprehend the Bible so you can be a sound, clear, and consistent teacher of God's Word to others."

Counterfeit currency is a real danger for a government. I'm told federal authorities study carefully to counteract any fraudulent money changers. Their primary study, however, is not on the fakes. Their primary task is to know the real currency so fully and so intimately that they are quickly able to see a fake when it appears.

There are many counterfeits of the truth in our world. Many people in our society are unaware of the truth, while others mix some of the truth with some error. And, sadly, many believers are too uninformed of the truth to spot the counterfeit.

Study God's Word so well that you are able to know the truth from the imitation. Know it is such a way that you speak only what is consistent with sound teaching. Especially in our day, consistency counts.

〜〜

Day Seven: Consistency Counts

Verse to Remember: Titus 2:1: "You must speak what is consistent with sound teaching."

Questions to Consider: Am I taking steps that will help me know the full truth of God's Word? What future steps will help me to be a sound teacher of the Bible? Why does understanding the consistency of the Bible matter?

Today's Bible Reading: John 13–14.

Chapter Two

FLOODING OVER: FINDING PERSONAL RENEWAL AND REVIVAL

Dry land can become cracked and unfruitful. Dry spiritual lives can become barren and lose vitality. God offers the refreshing spring of spiritual renewal and revival to those who turn to Him. Ask the Lord to send revival to your soul this week. As you study each day, ask the Lord to renew your spirit and passion so your life will overflow with the presence and power of the Lord.

The Power Source

You will receive power when the Holy Spirit has come
upon you, and you will be
My witnesses in Jerusalem, in all Judea and Samaria,
and to the ends of the earth.

ACTS 1:8

You have the power.

If you have trusted Christ as your Savior, you have access to the power needed to live successfully. God the Holy Spirit lives in you. And He is the source of power for living as God intends you to live.

It had been a whirlwind of emotions for the disciples. They were confused by the arrest and trial of Jesus. They were bewildered at the crucifixion. They were amazed at word of the resurrection. They were thrilled to spend those few weeks with Jesus afterwards. Now, they gathered as Jesus prepared to ascend back to the Father in heaven.

But Jesus commanded them to wait in Jerusalem. He told them, "You will be baptized with the Holy Spirit" (Acts 1:4–5). Then He told this gathering of disciples that the coming of the Holy Spirit would be the means of power by which they would witness to the world.

These were fishermen and tax collectors. They didn't come from privileged backgrounds. They weren't deeply educated. Their connections with the powers of the world were severely limited. Still, Jesus said that the coming of the Holy Spirit would give them the power to be witnesses around the world. The power they utilized was not from within themselves, but came from God Himself.

While education is a great thing, it isn't the most critical factor in fulfilling God's will for your life. Get all the education you can get, but don't think it can replace the power of the Holy Spirit. Financial security is helpful, but it certainly isn't the most important factor in following the Lord. Use your resources to do good things, but don't think of money as a replacement for the power of the Holy Spirit. Talents and abilities are wonderful. Develop them and use them. But never think that the skills you possess can replace the power of the Holy Spirit in your life.

The power of the Holy Spirit is more important to the success you have in God's work than anything else. The power of the Holy Spirit is the key to fulfilling the ministry and purpose for which God created you. It is the power by which God uses you to change the world.

⸻

Christians work better when they have power.

⸻

Plunging deeper in faith cannot happen without the filling of the Holy Spirit. Being filled with the Holy Spirit simply means that we are fully yielded to His will and His leading in our lives. It means that we operate under His influence; we follow His guidance.

The result of being filled with the Holy Spirit is a new power to share the good news and to witness of God's grace. A sign of being filled with the Holy Spirit is our boldness in witness. Acts 4:31 tells us, "They were all filled with the Holy Spirit and began to speak God's message with boldness."

When we allow God's Spirit to fill us, we receive God's power to do His work through us. The Holy Spirit is who empowers us to accomplish all God wants to do. We have the power of God living in us as believers, and God empowers us for service and witness.

I have a battery-powered weed cutter. It works great until the battery runs out. I guess I could still use it in some limited capacity. I could swing the whole thing around in a giant arc and smash it into the weeds, I suppose. But, let's face it; weed cutters work better when they have power.

Many Christians are trying to live their lives without the power to accomplish their purpose. They substitute ingenuity or religious activity for that which offers the only real power to do the job. They might get a few things done. But, let's face it: Christians work better when they have power.

The Holy Spirit wants to empower you for the difference-making life God created you to have. He wants to energize your service, motivate your ministry, and empower your witness. Without His power in your life, you may have lots of activity, but you will have few lasting results.

With the power of the Holy Spirit, fishermen and tax collectors, bankers and bakers, construction workers and schoolteachers, men and women, and boys and girls gain the ability to change the world. You need power to do what God wants you to do. Because God sent the Holy Spirit to live in you, when you give your life to Christ, you have that power. And He is all the power you need.

—∿∿—

Day Eight: The Power Source

Verse to Remember: Acts 1:8: "You will receive power when the Holy Spirit has come upon you, and you will be My witnesses in Jerusalem, in all Judea and Samaria, and to the ends of the earth."

Questions to Consider: Is the Holy Spirit able to use me in accomplishing God's work in the world today? Am I yielded to everything the Holy Spirit wants to do in me? Is there any area of my life that I am holding back from God? What do I know God wants from me right now?

Today's Bible Reading: John 15–16.

DAY NINE

Inside Information

The Spirit of God lives in you.

ROMANS 8:9

You have inside information.

Plunging deeper into faith is about more than changes in behavior. It's about more than the external. Discipleship is not merely a code of "dos" and "don'ts." Far too many have seen the Christian faith as merely a set of rules to keep. The gospel is much deeper than that.

Salvation is about a change on the inside. It is about people who were dead in their trespasses and sins coming to spiritual life in Christ (Ephesians 2:1–5). One becomes a new person through salvation in Christ (2 Corinthians 5:17). It is not just some outward adjustment; it is an inward rebirth.

The Holy Spirit lives in you and gives you inside information. You are not facing life's battles in your own strength. You are not going through life's journeys on your own. The Holy Spirit lives in you, so you can face every challenge and every opportunity with this inside information.

Knowing the Spirit of God lives in us is a powerful and life-changing truth. It is critical to our understanding of who we are and how we are to live. The eighth chapter of Romans teaches us more about this important concept.

We have inside information about forgiveness. We are told in the first two verses of Romans 8 that we are set free from" the law of sin and of death." The Spirit living in us reminds us that we now live under "the law of life in Christ Jesus." And, because of that, "no condemnation now exists for those in Christ Jesus."

What a thought: We are completely and fully forgiven in Christ. We no longer live under condemnation or shame or guilt. The Spirit, living in us, reminds us to appropriate this truth. We don't live under the burden of guilt. Our condemnation is completely and perfectly removed.

DOUG MUNTON

I meet believers all the time who are still carrying the burden of their past. Though the Lord Jesus forgave them of their sin when they trusted in Him, they still carry the shame and the guilt and the burden. It is so unwise and unnecessary. God does not intend for you to pick up the guilt of your past, which He has already fully forgiven. The Spirit of God in you reminds you to appropriate this truth about forgiveness of sin.

⸻

The Holy Spirit lives in you.

⸻

We have inside information about our relationship with God. Romans 8:14–17 teaches us the great lesson of relationship. Verse 14 says, "All those led by God's Spirit are God's sons." Verse 16 notes, "The Spirit Himself testifies together with our spirit that we are God's children."

What a truth! We are not only forgiven, we are also adopted into God's family. The Spirit of God is reminding us of this special relationship with God. He is not just a distant, far-removed sovereign. He is a loving and close father who has adopted us into His family. This gets to the very heart of the gospel message. We can have a close and intimate relationship with God.

We have inside information about the difficulties of life. Verse 18 tells us, "The sufferings of this present time are not worth comparing with the glory that is going to be revealed to us." While we will look at this verse in more detail next week, it is important to note that the Holy Spirit in us is reminding us that there is a greater glory to come. The problems in this fallen world can't compare to the promises of the heavenly world to come.

How grateful we should be for this promise. The Spirit of God lives in us. We have one who walks with us, leads us, and guides us. He points us to the truth and He helps us throughout the journey.

Along the path of life you will be tempted to give up. The enemy will whisper that following the path of discipleship is too hard, too steep, and too sacrificial. He will remind you of past failures and call you back to the old shackles of guilt and shame.

But you don't have to quit. You don't have to falter. You don't have to give in. You know something important and life-changing about your journey to full discipleship. The Holy Spirit dwells in you. You are not alone or left to do work in your own strength. The Bible tells you that the very Spirit of God lives in you as a believer—enabling you, empowering you, and encouraging you.

You have inside information—and that information makes all the difference.

⁓⁓⁓

DAY NINE: INSIDE INFORMATION

Verse to Remember: Romans 8:9: "The Spirit of God lives in you."

Questions to Consider: How does the presence of the Holy Spirit in my life change things? Is there a burden of past guilt that I need to trust God to forgive? Why is it important to understand God as my Father? Can I trust God's greater glory during my present problems?

Today's Bible Reading: John 17–18.

DAY TEN
Adjusting the Attitude

Make your own attitude that of Christ Jesus.

PHILIPPIANS 2:5

Attitude affects everything.

Do you ever have a rotten attitude? You probably know those days—the days when you are grumpy or irritated about every issue. Those are the days when your friends want to avoid you and your dog wants to find someone else's lap to sit on. We've all had them.

I've had enough of those grumpy, lousy attitude kinds of days that I even have a special name for them. I call them "Mondays."

I'm always tired on Mondays. The weekend is exciting for me. I get to preach and teach and mingle with lots of people. I love that. It is always a great joy and a frightening privilege to be allowed to preach the gospel to so many people. I'm up and excited and energized.

But, Monday is different. I'm tired and a bit drained. There are problems to deal with ("The toilet in the youth area overflowed again") and details to take care of ("Our best children's teacher is moving to Alaska"). I tend to have a bad attitude on Mondays.

Here is the surprising news about my bad attitude on Mondays. It isn't Monday's fault.

The truth is circumstances are not responsible for our attitudes. We are. Circumstances can certainly have an effect, but they don't have control. Did you notice how the Bible states that command? (And that it is a command?) "Make your own attitude," the verse says.

In other words, we have control over the attitudes we have. We "make" them. This is revolutionary stuff. Circumstances don't dictate our attitudes—we do.

My attitude does not need to remain a victim of anyone or anything else. I am not to blame wrong attitudes on bad drivers or poor parenting or unfriendly neighbors or spicy pizza or weedy flowerbeds or broken toaster pastries or anything else. My attitude is something I am to make.

It isn't made by my spouse or boss or dentist or senator. It is to be made by me.

～～ᶺ～～

Circumstances don't dictate our attitude.

～～ᶺ～～

And here is where it gets really revolutionary. I am to make my own attitude "that of Christ Jesus." That's a tall order indeed.

How thankful we should be that the Lord gives us an example to follow. He not only tells us the truth, He also shows us the truth. And the Lord has demonstrated the attitude we are to have.

The context of this verse concerns humility. Our attitude is to be like the Lord's attitude in every area of life. But this verse reminds us specifically about having a humble, servant-like attitude.

We have much to be humble about. We didn't save ourselves—we were incapable. We don't do the work of ministry—the Lord accomplishes His work through us by the power of the Holy Spirit. We are merely sinners who received unmerited grace and mercy. We have much to be humble about.

And our incredible, perfect Savior set the example. He "emptied Himself by assuming the form of a slave" (Philippians 2:7). He "humbled Himself by becoming obedient to the point of death" (Philippians 2:8). Though He had nothing to be humble about, He willingly humbled Himself to the point of washing the feet of His disciples and dying on a cross to pay the penalty for our sins.

That is the kind of attitude we are to have—humble, giving, and thinking of others. There is no room for pride in our hearts; no arrogance allowed. Pride is a dangerous attitude. It thinks that God is unnecessary and that one can make it by his or her own devices. It usurps the role of God and promotes a false image of ourselves and our abilities.

I am to choose, this day and the next, to have the kind of attitude that I see in the Lord Jesus. It is not to be based on my circumstances or difficulties. My attitude is to be based on my decision to follow Jesus and what He wants for me.

When we get our attitudes right, our actions tend to follow. We tend to do right when our attitude is right. When we think right, we tend to act right.

My attitude is to be right today—to be Christ-like, to be humble, and to be thinking of others and not myself. This day my attitude is to be that which resembles the selfless, giving attitude of my Savior. This day I am to think like the Lord thinks so I can do what the Lord does. My attitude is to be like that of Christ Jesus.

Even on a Monday.

—∽∼∽—

DAY TEN: ADJUSTING THE ATTITUDE

Verse to Remember: Philippians 2:5: "Make your own attitude that of Christ Jesus."

Questions to Consider: Has my attitude been less than Christ-like lately? Have I blamed my wrong attitudes on circumstances or others? Am I willing to take responsibility for my own attitude? Is there any pride in my life instead of the humble attitude exhibited by Christ Jesus?

Today's Bible Reading: John 19–20.

DAY ELEVEN

First Love

I have this against you: you have abandoned
the love you had at first.

REVELATION 2:4

Backslidden.

Few use the word today, but it paints a vivid portrait of what happens when our passion for God fades. We are sliding back from the Lord. If one's faith is growing colder rather than hotter, more shallow than deeper, we might well say that person is backslidden.

If revival could be thought of as a flood that drenches our soul, backslidden is the dry, cracked ground of a drought. But the act of backsliding—to use the word as a verb—is often rather subtle.

It might begin with the drying wind of ritualized prayer or lifeless worship. It might continue with the hardening drought of loveless ministry or compassionless service.

Jesus' words to the church of Ephesus, recorded in Revelation 2, frighten me. I look at the church in Ephesus and think everything is great. Jesus tells them, "I know your works, your labor, and your endurance" (Revelation 2:2). They show discernment (v. 2) and endurance (v. 3). I look at a church like that and think, *That is a fine church. Everything is great. They are active, they work, and they stick with it. It is a great church.*

But Jesus recognized the deepening problem they faced: Their passion for their Lord was cooling. They were backsliding.

We must be careful to recognize that God wants more from us than merely our "works, labor, and endurance." Activity begun to honor the Lord might well continue beyond the honoring. Hearts that once beat with passion for the things of God might now merely pump enough blood for us to make it to the next church meeting.

A believer who actively works, who faithfully attends, and who steadfastly remains might seem worthy of a medal to us. Yet those things

DOUG MUNTON

60

might be the shell while Jesus demands the heart. We say, "Everything is fine." He says, "I have this against you."

There is a remedy for the condition. Jesus counseled the backslidden church at Ephesus in the same way He would counsel us today. There are three things we must do to overcome the danger of a cold heart and a backslidden condition.

The first step in dealing with the problem is to remember. Jesus said to the church at Ephesus, "Remember then how far you have fallen" (Revelation 2:5).

A married couple struggling with disagreements and drifting toward isolation would do well to remember. They might remember those earlier times of budding romance. They could remember the happy times and the special moments. Focusing on those things that drew them together and made them one is a helpful step in rekindling dying love.

A part of remembering is the honest assessment of our spiritual lives. If we think all is well, we have no need for revival. But when we face the truth that our passion for the Lord has faded, then we can see the need for renewal.

Do you remember earlier days of deep passion for the Lord and His work? Was there a time when you longed to worship with other believers, hungered for His Word, and sought Him in prayer in a way that is greater than today? If so, you can see the need you have and how far you have fallen.

The second step toward recovering our first love is to repent. Repentance can never be erased from our theological dictionary if we desire intimacy with the Lord. It is a necessary component of real closeness with Him and with genuine dealing with our shortcomings.

⸻⸻

Repentance involves the changes in behavior or attitude required, and it leads to the renewal and revival desired.

⸻⸻

Repentance is more than remembering. You might know that you are backslidden but do nothing. Repentance is the act of doing something. It is a great and willing change in our actions or attitudes. It involves knowing what needs to be done and doing it. Repentance involves the changes in behavior or attitude required and it leads to the renewal and revival desired.

The third step the Lord calls us to take is to return. Jesus said, "And do the works you did at first" (Revelation 2:5). The Lord calls us to return to Him and enjoy the closeness and spiritual intimacy of that first love once again. This happens when we choose to no longer settle for religion without relationship or good works without great passion. It happens when we seek renewal of our soul and restoration of our heart.

Like the prodigal son who recognized his wrongdoing while in the pigpen and returned to the awaiting arms of his father (Luke 15), we return to our loving Heavenly Father who forgives and restores. We find once again the loving embrace of a Father who made us and saved us for spiritual intimacy and who longs for our passionate love in return. We find, once more, first love.

DAY ELEVEN: FIRST LOVE

Verse to Remember: Revelations 2:4: "I have this against you: you have abandoned the love you had at first."

Questions to Consider: Has there been a time when I was more passionate about the Lord and the things of the Lord? Is there any sense in which I am backslidden? Will the Lord restore and renew me if I seek Him with all my heart?

Today's Bible Reading: John 21; Proverbs 1.

Day Twelve
Heart Surgery

God, create a clean heart for me and renew a
steadfast spirit within me.

PSALM 51:10

Heart problems are serious.

I'm no doctor, but I think that first statement is pretty accurate when it comes to physical well-being. Okay, it doesn't take a genius to know that. But what is true of our physical health is doubly true of our spiritual health.

The condition of your spiritual heart—that which represents the very core of your being—is of great importance to the Lord and to the depth of your spiritual condition. When your heart is bad, all the bandages in the world are not enough. Heart issues are so important that they must not be ignored. They need our full attention and, where necessary, surgery by our Great Physician.

If your physical heart is diseased and your arteries are clogged, doctors will take serious steps. You may have to change your diet or behavior. You may need medication. You might even need some very significant surgery. Heart problems are to be taken seriously.

If your spiritual heart is diseased, if there is something wrong at the core of your soul, there are some important steps that need to be taken. The Lord always takes heart problems seriously.

Psalm 51 is an important message for those who want to plunge deeper in faith. David wrote this magnificent psalm, but not after a great victory. This psalm was not written during joyful worship or happy reflection on his relationship with the Lord.

David wrote this song of faith out of a broken heart.

David is called "a man after God's own heart" (Acts 13:22) and "a man loyal to Him" (1 Sam. 13:14). This describes the great passion he had for the Lord and the things of God. His love for God and His kingdom was deep and intense and strong. He followed the Lord bravely into battles and worshipped Him fully in life. His was a worship that was both intellectual and emotional, and the psalms he authored reflect that.

But this man who followed the Lord so passionately also failed the will of God spectacularly. From his rooftop one night, he saw a beautiful woman named Bathsheba bathing. Instead of guarding his heart and looking away, he fed his lust. Lust led to adultery. Adultery led to dishonesty and, eventually, to murder. His soft heart became hardened.

Confronted with his sin, David's heart was broken. He acknowledged his shameful acts and rebellious spirit. And he turned to the only Physician who can heal broken, sin-stained hearts.

David's response in Psalm 51 was what our response to sin must be if we are to experience healing: repentance. He pled with the Lord, "Wash away my guilt, and cleanse me from my sin" (v. 2). "Against You—You alone—I have sinned," he cries (v. 4). "Surely You desire integrity in the inner self," he acknowledged in verse 6.

This repentance led David to cry out for a clean heart and for renewal within his spirit. He recognized his sin, turned from it, and called out to the one who can forgive. There was no pretending that everything was okay, no masking the problems or running from the solution.

Only God can cleanse our hearts. He alone can make them new and remove the stain and the shame. He doesn't just hide our sin, He forgives our sin. He cleanses our hearts and He makes them new. He renews our spirit and brings us back to Himself.

Like David, we can return to the Lord. Even spectacular failure—sin that damages and disgraces—can be forgiven in repentance. The Great Physician still heals, still forgives, and still makes hearts new again.

⸺∿∿⸺

God cleanses our hearts and makes them new.

⸺∿∿⸺

I knew a man who had a heart attack. They discovered multiple blockages in his arteries. For a time he had ignored the symptoms instead of dealing with them directly. But a day came when they could no longer be ignored. Doctors performed life-saving surgery and the man recovered fully. He enjoyed many more years of time with family and service in his church and to His Savior.

There are many who need some spiritual heart surgery. They have grown calloused toward the work of the Lord or have strayed from obedience to His Word. Hearts that once beat to worship the King, now beat to serve their own appetites. There are blockages in their relationship with God and a hardening from their former tenderness and compassion and service.

Heart problems are never to be ignored. Whatever your need—whatever your problems—there is a Healer who can create a clean heart. There is a Savior who can renew a steadfast spirit.

The Great Physician still heals broken hearts today.

⸻

Day Twelve: Heart Surgery

Verse to Remember: Psalm 51:10: "God, create a clean heart for me and renew a steadfast spirit within me."

Questions to Consider: Is there something that is keeping me from a full relationship with the Lord? Have I sought and accepted the full forgiveness that comes through Jesus Christ? Is there some area of my life that needs repentance? Is my heart fully committed to the Lord?

Today's Bible Reading: Proverbs 2–3.

I Saw the Lord

Holy, holy, holy is the Lord of Hosts: His glory fills the whole earth.

Isaiah 6:3

Who is God?

Knowing who God is and what He is like is one of the most important aspects of plunging deeper into faith. God spends much of His Word describing who He is. He tells us who He is and isn't. He describes Himself in detail and tells us His characteristics. He distinguishes Himself from man's inaccurate views. We are shown His attributes and the details of His nature.

But one of the greatest descriptions of God in the Old Testament comes through a young prophet named Isaiah. He saw the Lord.

The Lord revealed Himself to Isaiah for our benefit as well as Isaiah's. Through Isaiah's vision of God we are able to see more of what God is like and who He is. And just as Isaiah benefitted from seeing God as He is, we can benefit from understanding more of who the Lord is.

⌒⌒⌒

God wants you to know Him.

⌒⌒⌒

The Bible tells us that man was created in God's image. But since the fall of mankind into sin, we have sought to recreate God into our image. God is God. He is not what we wish Him to be or think He ought to be or what our culture tries to make Him. He is God. And God reveals Himself to us because He wants us to know Him.

Let me say this more directly. God wants you to know Him. A relationship with God means you know Him closely, just as He knows you closely. You will never exhaust the subject of knowing God, but He wants to be known by you. And one of the most important parts of your growing faith will be your accurate, clear, thoughtful understanding of who the Lord is and what that means—to see the Lord.

Isaiah 6 tells us of Isaiah's life-changing experience. Isaiah said, "In the year that King Uzziah died, I saw the Lord seated on a high and lofty throne" (Isaiah 6:1). The prophet saw the majesty and glory of God. He was on a throne because He reigns as Sovereign. His throne was high and lifted up because the Lord is King of Kings and Lord of Lords.

The Bible goes on to tell us that His robe filled the temple and His voice shook the foundation. Seraphim—a type of angels—were attending Him and calling out to one another about the glory of the Lord (vv. 14). The sight must have been overwhelming to Isaiah. Never had he seen such spectacular things or witnessed so impressive a being.

The call of the seraphim is the focal verse for today. They called to one another, "Holy, holy, holy is the LORD of Hosts; His glory fills the whole earth." They describe to us what the Lord is like—His greatness, magnitude, and wonder.

Note the repeated description of the Lord as "holy." Without a full understanding of God's holiness, one does not know the Lord as He is and as He has revealed Himself to us. Holiness is descriptive of who God is and what He is like. It describes His nature and His activity.

We are told in His Word, "Be holy because I am holy" (Leviticus 11:44–45; 1 Peter 1:16). Our life is to be lived in holiness because it is the very nature of our great God.

And, therein lays the problem: He is holy and we are not.

The response of Isaiah to the awesome holiness of God was a resounding, "Woe is me, for I am ruined, because I am a man of unclean lips and live among a people of unclean lips" (v. 5). Seeing God's holiness highlighted the prophet's own ruined condition. God was holy, but Isaiah knew that *he* certainly was not.

One of our struggles with understanding our need for the Lord is our struggle to understand the nature of the Lord. When we see His holiness, we see our need. If we see God as something less than holy, we fail to see Him as He is, and we fail to see ourselves as needing His forgiveness or appreciating His mercy.

Isaiah continues by telling us about his volunteering for God's mission. He said, "Here I am. Send me" (v. 8). His willingness to do God's work was born out of his ability to see God's nature. Something of the same will be true of your service and ministry. The more you see of the true nature of our great God, the more willing you will be to give yourself to His work and service. Seeing Him as high and lifted up will lead you to a recognition of His worthiness.

The day might come when someone asks you why you are so faithful in obeying the Lord and why you spend so much effort in ministry and service. They might ask you why you volunteer to use your talents and abilities for the cause of Christ and why you are so willing to sacrifice for His purposes. And you might respond with a reason for your willingness that sounds much like Isaiah's reason: I serve and obey because I saw the Lord.

Day Thirteen: I Saw the Lord

Verse to Remember: Isaiah 6:3: "Holy, holy, holy is the LORD of Hosts; His glory fills the whole earth."

Questions to Consider: Am I fully aware of the holiness of God? Why does that matter to me? How does that motivate my service?

Today's Bible Reading: Proverbs 4–5.

Fruit Flavored

The fruit of the Spirit is love, joy, peace, patience,
kindness, goodness, faith, gentleness, self-control.

GALATIANS 5:22–23

The Spirit-filled life produces the fruit of the Spirit.

We had a prolific cherry tree in our yard when I was a teenager. It produced cherries by the thousands. I know this because it was my job to pick the cherries and remove the pits. While I didn't enjoy that part of the job much, I did enjoy the cherry pies and cobblers and jellies my mother made. So every summer I could be found with cherry juice dripping down my fingers and off my elbows as I busied myself with removing cherry pits from the delicious fruit.

⁓⌇⌇⁓

A fruit tree that doesn't produce fruit is missing the point.

⁓⌇⌇⁓

Cherry trees are to produce cherries. Fruit production is what fruit trees do. In a similar fashion, disciples of Jesus Christ are to produce fruit. The Bible calls it the fruit of the Spirit.

A fruit tree that doesn't produce fruit is missing the point. It might provide shade—and that is nice—but it is missing the intended results of its planting.

Plunging deeper into faith involves allowing the Holy Spirit to control one's life. And the Spirit-filled life has results. We can call these results "fruit" in that they are the intended result. Our lives are planted in the Spirit so they will bear the fruit of the Spirit. A believer who doesn't produce fruit is missing the point.

Nine attributes are mentioned as the fruit of the Spirit. Each of these deserves some careful consideration, as each attribute is what God wants every one of His followers to exhibit or produce.

The first fruit of the Spirit mentioned is love. No believer can be fully immersed in the message of the gospel without love as a hallmark of his or her life. Love is absolutely necessary and completely indispensable. But the problem is the application.

We are to love such unlovely creatures. We are to love sinners and saints, friends and enemies. This can only happen as we learn to love others in the same way the Lord loves us. His love, given to us on Calvary, must become our love, given to others freely.

The second fruit of the Spirit is joy. Joy is the deep-seated satisfaction that comes with following the Lord. It is more than just laughter; you can have joy even in the difficult moments of life. Circumstances do not determine joy. Your joy is found in your relationship with the Lord.

Peace is the third fruit of the Spirit. It is not the absence of the storm that brings peace. Peace is found in trusting the Lord in every situation and every circumstance. When we trust the Lord, we find Him to be trustworthy and He becomes the source of our peace. Our inner battles with sin and circumstances cease when we choose to trust the One who gives peace that passes understanding.

The fourth fruit of the Spirit spoken of is patience. We can trust the Lord's timing as much as His temperament. The closer I grow to the Lord and yield to the leading of the Spirit, the more I learn to trust His clock and to wait on His timing. I learn that He is not done working on me or others.

Fifth of the fruit of the Spirit is kindness. Rudeness is never of the Lord. God calls us to be kind to others and to consider them and their needs. Kindness is the choice to think of others and to do things that aid them. Kind people treat others as more important than themselves and think of the needs of others rather than their own needs.

Fruit of the Spirit number six is goodness. This attribute refers to our deeds done on behalf of others. Goodness is the desire to bless others. It springs from a heart of generosity and desires to be a blessing to someone else by doing something that is to their benefit. Goodness is willing to go the second mile when only one is required.

The seventh of the fruit of the Spirit is faith. A result of the Spirit-filled life is faith. We place our dependence on the Lord. We trust His provision and His leading and His direction. The life of faith knows that God is dependable and that He longs for us to prove Him in that area.

Eighth in the list of the fruit of the Spirit is gentleness. Gentleness is not weakness; it is strength under control. It manifests itself in humility rather than brashness and in consideration of others. Gentleness controls anger and malice and demonstrates grace under pressure.

The final of the nine aspects of the fruit of the Spirit is self-control. The Spirit-led life is disciplined. It is not given to out-of-control outbursts or a lazy or unproductive life. It takes responsibility for its own decisions, attitudes, and actions.

God planted you to bear fruit. Let the Spirit make you productive and prolific.

—〰〰—

DAY FOURTEEN: FRUIT FLAVORED

Verse to Remember: Galatians 5:22–23: "The fruit of the Spirit is love, joy, peace, patience, kindness, goodness, faith, gentleness, self-control."

Questions to Consider: Am I bearing the fruit of the Spirit? What is the hardest of these nine attributes for me? In which of these areas am I growing most?

Today's Bible Reading: Proverbs 6-7.

Chapter Three
TURBULENT WATER: FOLLOWING CHRIST IN DIFFICULT TIMES

Discipleship is not only for smooth, glassy waters. The Lord is Lord all the time—even when the waves are high. Plunging deeper into faith means we are willing to follow the Lord when the way is easy or difficult. Turbulent waters can bring lessons and opportunities the growing disciple will want to appropriate and seize.

DAY FIFTEEN
My Only Hope

Even if He kills me, I will hope in Him.

JOB 13:15

If you think you have problems...

Job was an amazing man with an amazing story of tragedy and triumph. Anytime I think my problems are great, I can remember the story of Job and my perspective is changed.

A man of great wealth, Job lost it all in a single day. All his financial security and all he had worked for was gone in a moment. His retirement plans were changed. Vacations were cancelled. Things once taken for granted were now luxuries.

Worse still, all of his children were killed in a storm on that same day. I cannot imagine the pain felt by Job and his wife. I cannot imagine their tears and their sorrow as they wept at the graves of their ten children. All the memories of happy days and all the joys of previous years could not console the deep ache of their broken hearts.

This was a man who lost everything he held dear. And then it got worse.

Job contracted painful boils on his skin from head to toe. Even the soles of his feet were covered. He couldn't walk without excruciating pain. Every movement of his body brought agony. His only hint of relief from the pain and the itch was to scrape himself with a broken piece of pottery.

The man who once had it all now found himself with nothing. The great businessman was broke. The great family man was childless. The man whose name was synonymous with power, fortune, and fame now found himself sitting in the ashes, seeking relief, which could never be fully attained.

His wife counseled him to curse the Lord so that the Lord might kill him and relieve him of his misery. Perhaps it was her grief and hurt talking, but Job found no comfort in those words. Friends came to speak with him. But their suggestions became primarily accusations against his character. Maybe they meant well, but their words brought more sting than healing.

DOUG MUNTON

78

Job lost everything—except for hope. He never lost hope, even in the terrible ordeals he faced, because his hope was never found in the things he possessed or the gifts he'd been given. His hope was found in the only source of lasting hope you or I will ever know. It was found in the person of his great God.

Through turbulent waters, Job continued to follow the Lord. His was not a "what's in it for me?" faith. His faith was not a way to find ease and comfort in life. His faith stood even when the flooding storms raged and the sky was as dark as night.

Plunging deeper into faith can mean swimming in some choppy waters. Our fallen world is filled with storms and difficulties. But deepening discipleship involves a deepening of our commitment to the Lord regardless of circumstances or comfort.

Serious discipleship has moved beyond "I'll follow you if . . ." That kind of shallow faith says, "Lord, I'll follow you if my life is comfortable. I'll follow you if my business deal goes through. I'll follow you if you remove all my problems." Job said, "I'll follow you." Note the placement of the period.

Our focal verse is Job's affirmation that his decision was not based on circumstances. He would follow the Lord wherever that led; even if that should lead to the grave. That is discipleship without looking back. That is something deeper, more serious and eternal. That is a commitment to a long walk in the same direction.

Perhaps you know the end of the story. Job had his fortune restored—even doubled. He and his wife had ten more children. His health was rejuvenated. But Job didn't know any of this when he spoke of his hope being found in the Lord. He didn't yet know if that hope would be fulfilled in this world or in eternity. He just knew that the Lord was the only hope this world will ever know.

⮕⮕⮕

Our hope is not that our problems will be absent, but
that our Lord will be present.

⮕⮕⮕

Discipleship may be revealed in circumstances, but it is never determined by circumstances. Through whatever difficulties come your way, the Lord provides the hope to go through them. He hasn't forgotten you or left you.

Plunging deeper into faith means our faith remains even when the waters we swim in are no longer calm. It means we trust the Lord when things are good, and we trust Him when things are bad. It means our hope is not that our problems will be absent but that our Lord will be present. Discipleship flows from the commitment of our heart and not the comfort of our health.

So, come what may—difficulties, loss, adversity, even death—we will hope in Him.

DAY FIFTEEN: MY ONLY HOPE

Verse to Remember: Job 13:15: "Even if He kills me, I will hope in Him."

Questions to Consider: What is so amazing about the story of Job? Has my faith deepened beyond, "Lord, I'll follow you if …"? Can I really trust God even when faced with storms?

Today's Bible Reading: Proverbs 8–9.

Through Dark Valleys

Even when I go through the darkest valley, I
fear no danger, for You are with me.

PSALM 23:4

Are you afraid of the dark?

Many times as a boy I laid awake in my bed in the dark. My mind raced to all the imaginary dangers, which seemed to lurk in every shadow. What if there were monsters in the closet? What if space aliens were hiding in the corner waiting under the cover of darkness?

In those moments of fear, it was helpful to have the reassurance of family. My father or mother could calm my fears by entering the room. All my anxieties began to melt away in their presence.

⁓⌇⌇⁓

If you live long enough in this life, you
will face some dark valleys.

⁓⌇⌇⁓

The psalmist knew something about darkness. This twenty-third psalm was written by David. And David knew something about dark valleys. He had the dark valley of rebellious children (one tried to take his throne and threatened his life), the dark valley of death of close friends and family, and the dark valley of trials and hardships. Maybe there weren't any monsters or space aliens, but his dark valleys were worse. They were real.

If you live long enough, you will face some dark valleys. They may come in the form of a broken heart, of deep grief, or economic hardship. But, in whatever shape they appear, they will come, and you will need to face them.

When facing a dark valley, we are reminded by the psalmist of two very important truths. Each of these truths is critical to a healthy understanding of the response of serious disciples to difficult times.

First, the psalmist reminds us that we are going "through" the darkest valley. We don't live in the darkness; we don't remain in the shadows. Dark valleys are not our homes. We pass *through* them.

Grief, loneliness, sorrow, and heartbreak are valleys that we pass through. These are not conditions that define us. They are not destinations where we put down stakes and pitch our tents. These are valleys that we pass through.

We can learn from our valleys. (And, by all means, we should learn from our difficult days.) It can take time to pass through these valleys. Valleys can be deep enough to leave us with scars that never fully heal until we reach the mountaintop of heaven. But, we do not abide in these valleys.

Second, we have company through these valleys. The follower of Christ never goes anywhere without the Lord's presence. Even the darkest days and deepest valleys are accompanied by the assurance of His companionship and comfort.

The presence of the Lord did not mean David was immune from dark valleys. It meant that David was immune from going through dark valleys alone.

It should be noted that this passage talks about the "darkest" valley. It isn't just any valley that is referred to, but the deepest, darkest, scariest valley imagined. This is the valley that is most difficult and the place at which we are most vulnerable.

And yet, even in that valley, David tells us that he doesn't live in fear. He isn't paralyzed or incapable of putting one foot in front of the other. His Companion will help him through even this greatest of difficulties.

As a pastor, I've been beside many men and women mourning the loss of a spouse. I've seen many bury a parent they deeply admired. I've watched too many mothers weep at the loss of a son or daughter. Those valleys can be so deep and so dark. It may seem as though they stretch on forever and that all hope must be abandoned.

But even in situations like those, I've seen the presence of God's Spirit providing comfort. I've seen the message of the gospel of hope provide peace. Often, in those moments, I've turned to the twenty-third psalm for truth and reassurance. And what powerful comfort these words have been.

If you live long enough, you will face one of these deepest of valleys. Or, perhaps you are in that valley right now. Know that the Lord is the One who walks beside you and comforts you on this journey through the valley. Though at times He can be awfully quiet, He doesn't leave you alone. You may not hear His voice, but you can trust His presence. You may not see His hand, but you can trust His heart.

This journey is another reminder of God's grace and tender compassion. He will guide you, comfort you, and help you through. You don't have to live in fear or be crippled by loneliness. He is right beside you.

Even in the dark.

—∿∿—

DAY SIXTEEN: THROUGH DARK VALLEYS

Verse to Remember: Psalm 23:4: "Even when I go through the darkest valley, I fear no danger, for You are with me."

Questions to Consider: Do I trust God as I go through my darkest valleys? How does knowing of God's presence help me when going through the darkest valleys? What was the darkest valley I've faced and what did it teach me about the Lord's nature?

Today's Bible Reading: Proverbs 10–11.

Midnight Opportunities

About midnight Paul and Silas were praying and
singing hymns to God,
and the prisoners were listening to them.

ACTS 16:25

Opportunities come at the most surprising times and places.

You might call it a bad day for Paul and Silas. It began, as it usually did, with Paul and Silas preaching and teaching. God even used them in a miraculous way to heal a slave girl who was demon-possessed. This miracle, however, was not well received by the girl's owners who had profited from her ability to tell the future.

When the owners saw that they had lost their profit-making ability, they grabbed Paul and Silas and dragged them before the magistrates. Soon a mob gathered. They demanded punishment for this loss of income and the magistrates concurred.

You might call it a bad day because Paul and Silas had their clothes stripped off and were beaten with "many blows" by rods. "Many blows" sounds unpleasant. Then, they were thrown into an inner prison and their feet were placed in stocks. Doesn't that sound like a bad day?

If you are beaten, thrown into prison, and placed in stocks for any reason, that sounds like a bad day. But when those things happen for doing the right things, it seems like an especially terrible day.

That makes our focal verse all the more amazing. At the end of this terrible day, Paul and Silas did something incredible. Instead of complaining and sulking and plotting revenge, they were "praying and singing hymns to God." They ended this day that seemed so terrible with a worship service.

Midnight is an opportunity to worship.

At midnight, after a long day of difficulties or trials or problems, worship might not be what we'd expect. Perhaps we might better expect tears and frustration and anguish. But midnight after a bad day is a great time for worship.

⸻〜〜〜⸻

Midnight is an opportunity to worship.

⸻〜〜〜⸻

Paul and Silas saw an opportunity that night. Tears might certainly have accompanied their singing. Cries for delivery probably accompanied their prayers. But worship was the opportunity of the hour. The Lord was still worthy to be praised. And midnight was a great time for worship.

On the night my father died, our family gathered in his room. After weeks of battling physical ailments, death was near. While we did not grieve as those who had no hope, we still grieved. And we sang.

As we circled the room where our family patriarch was dying, we sang hymns and choruses of faith. It felt like midnight in our souls, which made it a good time to worship. It is good to worship the Lord in the pleasant days and it is good to worship the Lord in the stormy nights. It is good to worship the Lord at noontime and it is good to worship the Lord at midnight. The Lord is worthy to be praised in all these moments.

There is a power to worship. It reminds us of who the Lord is. Notice, Paul and Silas sang to God. It was directed to Him. In worship we see more clearly who the Lord is. We sing of His greatness and His glory. We are reminded that He is worthy of our songs and our prayers.

If it feels like midnight in your soul, it is a good time to worship. Never is the time better for you to pray and sing. Tears may roll while you sing. Sobs may interrupt your prayers. But worship is needed at midnight. Your soul needs the refreshing perspective of worship. Your spirit needs the connection that comes only through prayer and singing. Midnight is an opportunity to worship.

Midnight is an opportunity to witness.

Notice the words of our focal verse. "And the prisoners were listening to them." I don't suppose they were used to other prisoners praising the

Lord. Singing hymns and praying must have seemed out of place in that dark prison.

And yet, there was a curiosity about the power behind such worship. What drove men to pray and sing instead of rant and rave? How could those men have such light in a place so dark? What did those men have that they didn't?

Midnight always brings opportunities to witness. We find that there are other prisoners and other people with problems. We have a new level of credibility and others have a new level of interest when it is midnight in a dark place.

While difficulties are real, so are our opportunities. We pray, "God, give me comfort and ease so I will have opportunities." The Lord replies, "Open your eyes to the opportunities around you right now—even in your difficulties."

Opportunities come at the most surprising times and places. Even at midnight in a prison cell at the end of a really bad day.

—⁓⁓—

DAY SEVENTEEN: MIDNIGHT OPPORTUNITIES

Verse to Remember: Acts 16:25: "About midnight Paul and Silas were praying and singing hymns to God, and the prisoners were listening to them."

Questions to Consider: Why is it important for me to worship during difficult times? In what ways might my actions in difficult times affect my opportunities to be a witness?

Today's Bible Reading: Proverbs 12–13.

DAY EIGHTEEN
Suffering Comparison

*The sufferings of this present time are not worth comparing
with the glory that is going to be revealed to us.*

ROMANS 8:18

We comparison-suffer like we comparison-shop. In comparison shopping, we compare one car to another car or one appliance to another appliance to see which one is the better deal.

In comparison-suffering we compare our problems to the problems of another. "Oh, you think your problems are bad? Yours are nothing in comparison to mine!" The problem is that we compare our suffering in the wrong way and to the wrong thing.

Paul knew something about suffering. He was beaten and imprisoned on multiple occasions. He was shipwrecked and faced trials and knew all about deprivation, hunger, and pain. When he wrote the words of our focal verse, he was imprisoned because of his faith.

He understood suffering. "Tribulation" could have been his middle name. Suffering he knew. But he also knew something about perspective.

When he compared his suffering to the sufferings of others, his suffering seemed intolerable. When he compared his suffering to the glory of the future, his suffering seemed trivial. If this world is all we have, our suffering is devastating. If there is the glory of eternity to come, our problems can be placed in perspective.

If you compare your problems to the problems of others, they can seem so overwhelming and so unfair. They can be devastating when compared to others. When we see our problems in the light of eternity and the promises of God, however, we see an entirely new angle.

A proper perspective of suffering teaches us two important things. First it teaches us that suffering is temporary. We live in a fallen world that is affected by the consequences of sin. Suffering is one of those consequences. But this world is not forever. This world, in fact, is not even our home.

DOUG MUNTON

Suffering needs a proper perspective.

When we travel, we might endure beds that are uncomfortable. We stay in the spare bedroom of a relative and sleep on a mattress that is old and sagging. We stay at a cheap hotel with a bed that is squeaky or lumpy. But we endure because we don't live there. It isn't the comfortable, familiar bed of home. We are on a journey, but we are going home.

This world is not our home. We are passing through on this journey of life, but it isn't home. We don't like the sufferings, the difficulties, and the problems. But we know that we aren't home yet. And one day we will be home—where there is no more suffering. There will be no more tears, no more sorrow, and no broken hearts or bodies.

A proper perspective also teaches us that heaven is far greater than our difficulties. The two are not worth comparing, the Bible tells us. We lose sight of this if we see heaven as less than the glorious home it is. If it is merely a place that beats the alternative but seems awfully boring, we don't recognize the Lord's magnificent plan. Heaven is far greater than we have realized.

I first saw the ocean as a college graduate. Not having any oceans in my home state of Illinois, I had never seen one in person. I had seen many ponds and small lakes, of course, and that was my standard of comparison.

In person, the ocean was far greater than my imagination. I could not believe how vast and how powerful it was. I couldn't get over the vivid hues of blue and green and white. Puffs of ocean spray amazed me. The roar of the crashing waves on the unyielding rocks delighted me. I was shocked by how salty the water tasted and how the undertow tugged at my feet.

The ponds of my past were not worth comparing to the glory that was revealed to me in the ocean's majesty. They suffered in comparison.

Perspective teaches us that the difficulties of our present lives are nothing in comparison to what God has in store for us in heaven. The glory of the home He has prepared for us is greater than anything this world can offer. And, it is greater than anything this world can take away.

Our focal verse calls us to a better perspective. We don't ignore our problems; we put them in proper perspective. We compare them, not with the problems of others, but with the promises of eternity. Seen in that light, there is no comparison.

With that perspective, a man sitting in prison for the crime of following Jesus Christ can write words of hope and comfort. With that perspective, one dealing with problems that seem insurmountable to others can find passion and purpose. Difficulties become opportunities; prison cells become choir halls.

What are our problems in light of heaven's glory? There's just no comparison.

━⌇∿⌇━

Day Eighteen: Suffering Comparison

POINTS TO PONDER

Verse to Remember: Romans 8:18: "The sufferings of this present time are not worth comparing with the glory that is going to be revealed to us."

Questions to Consider: Where has my perspective of my difficulties been right or wrong? Have I considered the greatness and glory of heaven sufficiently? How might that help me?

Today's Bible Reading: Proverbs 14–15.

Those Who Mourn

Blessed are those who mourn, because they will be comforted.

MATTHEW 5:4

"I've cried so much I don't have any tears left."

Those were the words a woman said to me at the funeral of her dearly loved family member. Many can identify with her sentiments. If we live long enough, we will all understand what it is to mourn. If we live long enough, we will walk through the grief of the death of loved ones.

Do you remember the first funeral service you attended? Perhaps it was for an older relative—a great-grandparent who had been ill or a great-uncle you hardly knew.

For some, the first funeral they attended was much more personal. It might have been for a dearly loved grandparent. Or it might have been the funeral of a parent or a sibling or a close friend. Perhaps it was a time of terrible loss, and deep, soul-wrenching sorrow.

The Bible says, "You will not grieve like the rest, who have no hope" (1 Thessalonians 4:13). It isn't that we don't grieve. Of course we experience the loss, the pain, and the separation. It is that we don't grieve in the same way as those who have no hope.

Our grief over the death of those who know Christ as Savior is tempered by the promise of God's forgiveness and salvation. We have assurance that Jesus is willing and able to forgive sin. We see His power over sin on the cross and over death in the empty tomb. For the believer, where death and sorrow and grief exist, hope abounds.

The words of Jesus in our focal passage must have grabbed the mind and heart of many who listened to Him on that hillside long ago. Many of them were grieving. There must have been mothers and fathers listening that day who had cried out in anguish over the death of an infant son or daughter. Many had lost a brother or sister, a mother or a father. They were those who mourn.

DOUG MUNTON

And Jesus called them "blessed." The word used here could well be translated "happy."[1] Imagine how odd that must have sounded. Mourning is really something you can be happy about, Jesus told them.

Does it sound odd to connect happiness and grief? How could Jesus say such a thing? Because He knew the reason the two seemingly incongruent concepts can be connected. That reason is the comfort that can only come from Him.

⚬⌁⌁⌁⚬

For the believer, where death and sorrow and
grief exist, hope abounds.

⚬⌁⌁⌁⚬

Jesus promises the grieving widow, the broken-hearted parent, and the weeping orphan access to His comfort. He reminds us in our pain and sorrow and fear that we can find comfort in His presence and in His promises.

Having gone through a time of grief and loss recently, I know more than I ever have about the comfort of the Lord. I know that the pain and separation of death are real. But I also know that the comfort that comes from the Lord is real. Sometimes the comfort comes through loving friends or a caring church. Sometimes the comfort comes through the still, small voice of God in the middle of the night when no one else is around.

I have found no greater comfort than in knowing the promises of God concerning eternity. The Bible makes the great and comforting promise that death is not the end for the believer. In fact, while it brings separation from those who remain behind, death will mean the greater joy of God's presence and of enjoying the home we were created and saved to experience.

The more I understand about heaven, the greater my excitement about being there. Far from being a dull, tedious place, it is described in the Bible as a place which is exciting and full of adventure, joy, and dis-

---

[1] A.T. Robertson, *Word Pictures in the New Testament* (Nashville: Broadman Press, 1930) Volume 1, pp. 38–39.

covery. It is the place your soul is longing to experience if you know Christ as your Savior.

I have found joy in knowing that those who die in Christ before me are in heaven and that one day I can see them again. I can picture myself singing praises to my Savior (with a much better voice, I might add) in the presence of friends and family who have gone before me.

What a comfort it is to think that I will see some in heaven with whom I have had a very special relationship. I will have been the one God used for them to hear the message of the gospel. Or, perhaps I will have been one who helped them in their journey of discipleship.

Yes, happiness can be connected to mourning. Those who grieve can find comfort in the Lord. The promises of God are real in every circumstance of life. The Lord's comfort is available to us. We can find happiness and hope again.

Even when we've cried until we can cry no more.

—∽∾∿∾—

DAY NINETEEN: THOSE WHO MOURN

Verse to Remember: Matthew 5:4: "Blessed are those who mourn, because they will be comforted."

Questions to Consider: In what ways can I find happiness even when I mourn? Do I know someone who needs the comfort of the Lord? How might God use me to help someone who is mourning?

Today's Bible Reading: Proverbs 16–17.

Comfort Paid Forward

He comforts us in all our affliction, so
that we may be able to comfort those who are in any kind
of affliction, through the comfort we ourselves receive from God.

2 Corinthians 1:4

We can focus so much on the *promise* of God's comfort that we forget
the *purpose* of God's comfort.

Materialism tells us that we get so that we can have. Much of our
culture has bought into that wrong viewpoint. The goal of our society
often becomes accumulation. When our goal is to get, there is never
enough. We will never be satisfied. There is always something more we
must have.

~~~

We can focus so much on the *promise* of God's comfort
that we forget the *purpose* of God's comfort.

~~~

The Lord corrects us and shows us the truth: We get so we can give.
Having things is not an end in itself. Those things will end. They aren't
eternal or lasting. The Lord gives to us so we can give. Giving is the
reminder that things are not eternal. It is a reminder of those things that
last and those things of greatest value.

The materialistic mind-set can apply to our comfort in our affliction.
We are not comforted merely for the purpose of having comfort. We are
not comforted just so we can have comfort just as we are not given material things so we can accumulate them. We are given so we can give. We
are blessed so we can bless. We are comforted so we can comfort.

It is easy to forget others during times of affliction. We can easily
become so focused on our own problems that we lose sight of the problems

others face. We pray for God's comfort, and rightly so. We understand-ably ask for God's blessings. But God grants that comfort and those bless-ings for something more than our attainment of them. He gives them to us so that we can be a means of giving them to others.

When I find the peace of God in the middle of the storm, it isn't just so that I can enjoy the peace. It is given to me so that I will help another find that same peace. When I find the loving embrace of my Heavenly Father during grief, it isn't just so that I can bask in His grace. It is given to me so I can help another find that same embrace of the Father.

My blessings are given to me as a means by which the Lord blesses others through me. I become a conduit of God's blessings to others. My recognition of His blessing allows me to bless others in His name. The purpose in my receiving comfort includes giving comfort to others.

The greatest helpers to me in affliction tend to be those who have already gone through the same (or similar) affliction. They have an understanding and an empathy that allows them to show me how God has blessed them and how He can bless me. Some know *about* the anguish of divorce or the heartbreak of rebellious children or the pain of addiction. Others know those emotions from personal experience. Some can talk to us *about* God's comfort. Others comfort us with the comfort they have already received from the Lord.

During seminary days, I had a professor who had lost his wife to ill-ness a couple of years earlier. He often took detours from his lectures to teach us life lessons every bit as important as the assigned subject. He told us that after her death, he often had well-meaning people talk to him about the comfort of the Lord that they knew he would find. Of course, they spoke the truth. But they didn't understand. It was a truth they knew—not a reality they had known.

Others, however, impacted the life of my professor in greater ways. They talked about the comfort they found in the Lord following some journey through terrible affliction. They spoke, not of what they had read, but about what they had experienced.

And they were paying their comfort forward.

We are to pay our blessings forward. Someone else needs the bless-

ings we have been given. Someone else needs the comfort we have discovered. Going through affliction? Perhaps God wants to use you in the
lives of others going through affliction. Perhaps He wants you to be the
conduit by which another discovers the loving embrace or powerful
peace He has for them.

We should never forget the promise of God concerning His comfort
in our time of need. It is a great and important promise. But we ought
never to forget that the promise comes with a purpose. The Lord has
comforted us so that we will comfort others. There is someone who
needs to know that same assistance we have discovered. Now, let's start
paying that comfort forward.

≈≈≈

Day Twenty: Comfort Paid Forward

Verse to Remember: 2 Corinthians 1:4: "He comforts us in all our affliction, so that we may be able to comfort those who are in any kind of affliction, through the comfort we ourselves receive from God."

Questions to Consider: Have I been focused only on the promise of God's comfort, forgetting the purpose of God's comfort? Is there someone I know who needs the comfort from afflictions I have found in God? Can I be a conduit of God's blessing to another?

Today's Bible Reading: Proverbs 18–19.

Your Greatest Supporter

Cast your burden on the Lord, and He will support you.

PSALM 55:22

Tom Johnston was heavy.

It was spring football practice at my college and the coach had us involved in all kinds of conditioning drills. One of the most arduous was a drill where we ran up the steps of the stadium—with someone on our back. I chose Tom Johnston.

Tom was a muscular, large lineman. I was a scrawny defensive back determined to get stronger. So, I chose to carry Tom on my back up the stadium steps over and over. Might that have something to do with my back problems today? Maybe those two things are merely coincidental.

Sometimes our problems are bigger than we can carry. We are unable to bear the weight or carry the burden. They drag us down and break our will. No matter how big or how strong we are, there are some burdens too great for us to carry on our own backs. And the Lord does not intend for us to carry these burdens ourselves.

Fortunately, there is one who can support us. There is one who is big enough and strong enough to carry our burdens up the steepest hills. No problem we face is too great for Him. The Lord is able to bear any weight we give to Him.

Perhaps you are carrying a burden. It might be the burden of shame. You've been trying to carry the shame of past events and that burden is too great for you. There is no sin too great for the Lord to forgive. There is no wrong done to you that the Lord cannot heal. Shame is never a burden you must carry on your shoulders.

You might be carrying another kind of burden. You might carry the burden of loss or separation. Perhaps you have gone through a painful divorce. You may carry the burden of a broken friendship or a broken family. No loss is too great for the Lord to bear. You are not intended to carry these weights on your shoulders through the course of life.

DOUG MUNTON

The Lord is able to bear any weight we give to Him.

⸺∿〜⸺

Some carry the burden of regret. "If only" becomes their motto. They carry a burden because of a missed opportunity or a wrong decision at a critical time. They look back with regret and carry that heavy burden through life. But the burden is too great. The past cannot be remade. The Lord wants to carry the burden that is too great for a person to bear.

Not only is He our greatest support in the sense that He can carry our burdens, but the Lord is also our greatest supporter in another sense. No one is a greater encourager and cheerleader for us in our race of life. The Lord cheers us on louder and longer than anyone.

On Saturdays during football season, that same stadium, which had earlier been a tool of training, was filled with football fans. They cheered us on and applauded our efforts. Some days we gave those fans more to cheer about than others, but they were faithful supporters who wanted our victory. Their encouragement meant so much to us.

No one will ever cheer for you as passionately as the Lord. He invites you to give all your cares and burdens to Him because He is completely for you and wants you to experience victory. He cheers for your successes and urges you to move beyond your defeats. He is for you.

Our focal verse tells us to "cast" our burden on the Lord. It is an act that we are to perform. The Lord already knows about our burdens. He waits for us to be willing to give those burdens to Him. He waits for us to trust Him with those burdens instead of carrying them ourselves.

The question for us is whether or not we trust Him with these burdens. Do we trust that He can handle our problems? Do we believe that He is willing to take these broken dreams or these worries that consume us or the issues that crush us? Is He able and is He trustworthy to take these problems that we have so unsuccessfully tried to carry ourselves?

Note that the verse tells us that "He will support you." It doesn't say that He might support you; it says that He will. It's a promise.

I can cast all my burdens upon the Lord. I can trust His ability to handle these problems, and I can trust His heart to care about them. I merely cast them upon Him because I trust Him with the problems that I face.

Even when they weigh more than Tom Johnston.

Day Twenty-One: Your Greatest Supporter

POINTS TO PONDER

Verse to Remember: Psalm 55:22: "Cast your burden on the LORD, and He will support you."

Questions to Consider: What burdens am I carrying right now? Do I believe God is able to handle those burdens? Is He trustworthy to handle them? Am I willing to cast those burdens upon Him right now?

Today's Bible Reading: Proverbs 20–21.

Chapter Four

POURING RAIN: RECOGNIZING BLESSINGS AND BLESSING OTHERS

God has blessed us in more ways than we realize. Plunging deeper into faith involves appreciating those blessings and using them as a means of blessing others. It means we have a thankful spirit that causes us to be a blessing to others as well.

Count Your Blessings

Give thanks to the Lord, call on His name; proclaim
His deeds among the peoples.

Psalm 105:1

The more blessings my father counted, the more he remembered.

My father served in the armed forces during the Korean Conflict. Army life was difficult. He was far from home, far from comfort, and far from safety. Food was often bad; sleep was often scarce; and hope was often limited.

Growing up on the farm had its trials, but nothing like his time in Korea. Working in construction was difficult, but nothing like what he faced in war. He was homesick, tired, and, I would guess, a little scared.

But as difficult as Dad's time in combat was, it became a time of great spiritual growth and lasting commitment. Everything changed for him in one day as he sat on a hilltop in the mountains of Korea. That hilltop became his cathedral and my father conducted important business with God that day. The course of his thinking, his future, and his life were changed by what happened there.

It started during a time of rest from the rigors of battle. Sent back to the safety of the rear for some rest and relaxation, Dad decided to get away from everyone for a day and climb a nearby hill where he could think and pray. But what he did next was life-changing.

There on that hill, my father did something unexpected. He began to count his blessings. There is an old song that said "Count your blessings, name them one by one. Count your many blessings; see what God hath done." That is what he began to do.

Counting your problems is more common than counting your blessings, I'm afraid. We often pray by listing for God all our difficulties, needs, shortages, and problems. And I'm glad we are able to bring those needs to God. But what a perspective change it is when we begin to count our blessings.

DOUG MUNTON

Should you do that, you might discover the same phenomenon my father discovered on the hillside in Korea. The more you count, the more you remember.

≈≈≈≈≈

The more blessings you count, the more you remember.

≈≈≈≈≈

He remembered long-forgotten blessings remembered on that hillside. Ignored blessings that were given day by day came flooding to his mind. Little things, common things, big things, and extraordinary things began to join the growing list of blessings. While his problems were real, he was reminded that his blessings were just as real—and more numerous than he realized.

Instead of focusing on all his problems and trials, my father began to focus on the multitude of blessings he had received. His faith was renewed. His joy was restored. God even used that day to confirm his call into vocational ministry. Dad went up the hillside tired, drained, beaten, and worried. He came down invigorated, renewed, and filled with purpose. Counting your blessings has a way of doing that to a person.

I'm asking you to do an important assignment today. Take some time to count your blessings. I'm not asking you to ignore your problems. Rather, I'm urging you to gain some perspective and insight by counting the ways God has blessed you.

Take a sheet of paper and begin writing blessings you have received from God. Some will come easily; then a lull will follow. Slowly but surely, you will begin to remember blessings. Your pace will quicken. Long-forgotten blessings will reemerge. Things taken for granted will become items for which you offer praise to the Lord. A mind that has been programmed by the world to focus on problems will begin to refocus on blessings. This may well be the most important of this 40-day experience for you.

His time on the hilltop was a lasting practice for my father. When he passed away, his last weeks were still focused on the blessings and on praising his Savior and Lord. He was still telling others about the Lord's blessings and still remembering all the gifts the Lord had provided.

After my father's death, I was going through photographs with my mother. She showed me a picture of my father taken during his army days in Korea. He was standing in his army t-shirt, his shirt swung over his shoulder. He had a happy smile, and I was glad to see him as he had once been—young and vibrant and full of life.

My mother pointed out something in the background. It was a hill. "That," she said, "was the hill where your father counted his blessings." We both knew what that meant—what God had done in our loved one's life in that difficult time. It was a special place for him and a special place for our family.

Today is a good day for you to count your blessings. Maybe it seems like a terrible time. You feel like you're in a battle with enemy soldiers all around. But today is a great day to count your blessings. Name them one by one. And it will surprise you what the Lord has done.

Day Twenty-Two: Count Your Blessings

Verse to Remember: Psalm 105:1: "Give thanks to the Lord, call on His name; proclaim His deeds among the peoples."

Questions to Consider: Take out a notebook or sheet of paper and write a list of blessings you have received from the Lord. Answer this question, "In what specific ways has God blessed me?"

Today's Bible Reading: Proverbs 22–23.

Saying Thank You

But one of them, seeing that he was healed, returned and,
with a loud voice, gave glory to God.

Luke 17:15

Ten men were healed, but only one returned to thank Him.

On His way to Jerusalem, Jesus passed through a particular village. At a distance, ten men raised their voices, crying out for mercy. They suffered from a serious skin disease and, therefore, were not allowed to live in a town. The law required that they stay away from healthy people lest they spread their contagion. So, they cried out from a distance.

Can you imagine their pain? They were no longer allowed access to their wives or children. No longer could they sip a hot drink with friends at a first-century version of the coffee shop. They couldn't attend birthday parties or watch their nephews and nieces play sports. They weren't invited to a friend's home or allowed to babysit a grandchild. They could only huddle together with others who suffered as they did and watch the years of their lives pass by.

Can you imagine their hope? They heard about a man—a very special man—who healed the blind and even the leper. Can it be true? Is there really a chance? Can such things really happen? Around the fire at night, they must have asked questions like these and dreamed of things they had not dreamed of for a very long time.

One day, to their astonishment, Jesus happened to come near their camp as he headed to the nearby village. They "raised their voices" the Bible tells us—and we can certainly believe that. Their voices must have squeaked in hope; their larynxes strained with passion. They cried out to the only opportunity they knew, "Jesus, Master, have mercy on us!"

The plea for mercy is interesting. Mercy is not getting what we deserve. When we get the things we have earned or the things we deserve, that is not mercy. Mercy is, by definition, getting the love that we do not deserve. Apparently, they were not asking for healing because they felt they deserved it. Rather, they asked for that which they did not deserve. They asked for mercy.

Jesus told the ten men to follow the commandment of the Bible and show themselves to the priests. But an amazing thing happened. While they were going, they were healed. Their disease was cured, their stigma was removed, and their hope was restored.

But, only one came back. Jesus noted this. He asked the one who returned, "Where are the nine?" Why did the others not return to thank the Lord? Why only this one man?

—————

Many fail to recognize blessings because
they see those blessings as something they deserve.

—————

Many fail to recognize blessings because they see those blessings as something they deserve. We don't thank the neighbor for returning our ladder that we allowed him to borrow.

Is it possible that the other nine men did not thank Jesus for healing them because they believed He owed them something anyway? Did they call for mercy while secretly believing it was something they deserved? The one who returned was a Samaritan. Is it possible the others had grown up closer to faith and felt they were owed something by God?

Perhaps they had an entitlement mind-set: "I deserve every blessing that comes my way. God owes me something." May I remind you that we do not want what we deserve? According to God's Word, as sinners we deserve death and hell and judgment. We certainly don't want what we deserve; we want mercy instead.

Did the nine just forget to express thankfulness? After all, their minds must have been jumbled with things to do. "Who will I see first? I can't wait to kiss my baby girl! Oh, how I look forward to sleeping in my own bed again!"

Many of us are so busy we seldom stop to express thanks to our

Savior. If you completed the assignment from yesterday to count your blessings, perhaps you were amazed at how many things you had forgotten to thank the Lord for doing for you. Maybe you were surprised at how seldom you thanked Him or the blessings you have failed to notice.

But one man came back. He gave glory to God "with a loud voice." The Bible tells us he fell facedown at the feet of Jesus and began to thank Him. There was no entitlement mind-set in this one. He wasn't too busy to return nor too proud to worship. This was one grateful man.

One man returned to give thanks. One man returned to acknowledge the Lord's goodness and mercy. One man fell at His feet in appreciative worship.

Often the crowd is too busy or too foolish to give thanks. But you can be that one man or one woman or one teenager or child who gives thanks to the Lord for what He has done for you. Today is a good day to give thanks and to remember the One who healed you from sin and removed the stigma and stain of wrongdoing. Today is a good day to fall at His feet, give glory to God, and worship.

Even if you give thanks alone.

Day Twenty-Three: Saying Thank You

Verse to Remember: Luke 17:15: "But one of them, seeing that he was healed, returned and, with a loud voice, gave glory to God."

Questions to Consider: Do I have a thankful spirit? Why are some people more thankful than others? Do I have an entitlement mind-set? How has counting my blessings changed my attitude?

Today's Bible Reading: Proverbs 24–25.

Thanks for the Memories

I give thanks to my God for every remembrance of you.

PHILIPPIANS 1:3

We have a special connection with other believers.

Years ago there was a television commercial that caught my attention. It showed a construction worker whose hard hat was glued with a special adhesive to a metal I-beam. The man was holding on to his hard hat, dangling from the bottom of the I-beam with his feet dancing in the air. It was an effective way of showing the powerful nature of the glue.

Believers have a special adhesive with each other. We are bonded together by our common faith, common mission, and common Father. That bond is powerful and important. It can be deeper than common backgrounds and even than common ancestry. It can be lasting and meaningful and a vital part of our spiritual development.

Paul had a special connection with the church in Philippi. He was part of the planting of that church. He was part of their heritage and legacy. There was a personal connection of friendship and a spiritual connection of faith. They had served together and sacrificed together. The Philippian church prayed for Paul and Paul prayed for them. They loved him and he loved them.

You can see this special bond in the letter to the Philippians. It is personal and encouraging. The connection of faith is obvious and strong. This is more than a form letter; it's personal.

Our focal verse reminds us of the great gift of memories given to us by the Lord. Paul, writing this letter from prison, must have thought back frequently to those special days he enjoyed with the church in Philippi. What joy those memories brought to him. He remembered the laughter and the tears, the hard work and the relaxation, the painful setbacks and the hard-won victories. Memories were a special gift to him in that dark prison cell.

On occasion you may look back at old photographs or reminisce with someone about bygone days. It's interesting what stands out to us in those moments. We remember people who loved us and people who taught us. We remember some old hurts, and we especially remember sweet times.

Most of our memories seem to revolve around people—the connections we've made, the people who have loved us or helped us, or those who have showed us love and compassion.

The importance of connecting with other believers is devalued today. Churches are often seen as unimportant. Small groups are believed to be unnecessary. Close friendships with other believers are deemed irrelevant. And the need for accountability or mutual support in discipleship is virtually nonexistent in many places.

I suspect we devalue church and small groups and close friendships with other believers because those other people are so—well, they are so human. People are sinners and they are messy and they are so very imperfect. Connecting with them means we are connecting with people who are less than ideal—kind of like we are.

But God made us with a need for each other. And, to our great surprise, we often find how many of the blessings of life we enjoy come through the hands of other sinful and imperfect people. We find that they are a great blessing to our lives even though they are less than ideal. And we find our lives so much richer because others have bonded with us in this journey of faith and discipleship.

Do you think the church at Philippi was perfect? Of course not. But, sitting in a prison cell writing a letter of encouragement to that imperfect church, Paul could not help but remember all the great blessings he had received in life through the people there. Every time he thought of them, he thanked his God. They had been a source of great blessing to his life.

⸺⁓⁓⸺

God made us with a need for each other.

⸺⁓⁓⸺

Get involved in the life of some other imperfect believers. Get active in your church and small groups and accountability or ministry connections. Build some memories of service and work and sacrifice together. Help them through their hard times and good times. Learn with them, pray with them, and grow with them.

You just might find the connections you make to be some of your greatest joys. You may well look back one day at this time of ministry and say how thankful you are to God for those people who joined you in this season of life. It may be that your church family or small group or men's bible study or women's prayer circle will be the source of great thanksgiving as you remember back years from now.

And you may find that God has blessed you through others so that you will be a blessing to someone else.

—∽∿∿∽—

Points to Ponder

Verse to Remember: Philippians 1:3: "I give thanks to my God for every remembrance of you."

Questions to Consider: Why does God place such emphasis on being connected with other believers? Am I actively pursuing relationships with other Christians? Am I helping anyone else grow in their faith? Do I need a deeper commitment to my church or small group?

Today's Bible Reading: Proverbs 26–27.

Saying Grace

Devote yourselves to prayer; stay alert in it with thanksgiving.

COLOSSIANS 4:2

"God is great. God is good. Let us thank Him for our food."

When we bow our heads before a meal and thank God for our food, we often call that "saying grace." While it can be merely a habit or duty, saying grace is really our way of acknowledging the blessings God has given to us. We use it as a way of reminding ourselves that our food and our blessings come from the Lord. It is a means by which we give thanks to God for His gifts to us.

The attitude of prayer, however, ought to extend far beyond a meal. It should certainly be something more than a ritual. Prayer is a vital part of our discipleship process. It is an important aspect of our connection with the Lord. It is a necessary component of healthy spiritual growth.

Our focal verse today teaches us three important lessons about prayer. First, it tells us to devote ourselves to this task. Prayer is not an afterthought or a last resort. Prayer is to be something to which we are devoted.

The word "devote" carries the idea of "persisting in" prayer. That is, prayer is not just an occasional practice. Rather, prayer is to be a deep commitment of our lives.

As a husband, I am to be devoted to my wife and my marriage. I'm not a part-time husband. Marriage is not to be something I'm devoted to only on anniversaries and birthdays. My devotion is evidenced by my faithfulness, my commitment, and my attitude. The things I do for my wife, the way I treat her, and the energy I pour into our marriage are all areas that demonstrate my devotion.

What if I never talked to my wife? What if I just ignored her or never spent time with her? Wouldn't you wonder about my devotion?

What if I never talk to my Lord? What if I ignored Him or never spent time with Him in prayer or devotions? Wouldn't it be fair to wonder about the level of my devotion?

DOUG MUNTON

One of the purposes of the 40-day devotional experience of *Immersed: 40 Days to a Deeper Faith* is to begin to develop a pattern of "devoting ourselves to prayer." By spending time each day reading the Bible and devotionals and considering the application, we begin to develop a deeper commitment to spending time with the Lord in prayer.

A second thing our focal passage teaches us about prayer is that we are to "stay alert" in it. This might be translated "being watchful" in prayer. The idea is that we are fully engaged in the activity of talking to God in prayer. We are awake and alert and engaged.

May I be honest with you? There are times when my prayers have been more habit than substance. I have found myself "praying" without my mind fully participating. I'm saying words, but I'm praying little.

On other occasions, my mind has been fully engaged. In those moments, I have poured my heart out to God with a greater urgency and passion. These are no rote prayers; these are heart-felt, soul-searching, mind-concentrating discussions and supplications. I've talked to God earnestly and known the close connection that comes with intimate prayer.

That is the kind of prayer the Lord wants from us. In alert prayer, we seek the Lord and we grow deeper in our walk with Him. In alert prayer we see the privilege of praying for others and for our own needs. In alert prayer, we are talking with our Father with a deeper level of closeness. Watchful prayer is connected and earnest and passionate.

A third aspect of prayer taught by our focal verse is thanksgiving. We are told to be devoted to prayer and to be alert in it and we are to do these things with a thankful attitude.

⤳∿∿⤶

Plunging deeper into faith always involves
a deepening commitment to prayer.

⤳∿∿⤶

Always our prayer is to include a level of thankfulness. We are always to acknowledge the blessings we have received. Even when we are pouring out our requests to the Lord, we are to thank Him for the blessings already received. When our prayers are filled with confession and repentance, they still carry the message of gratefulness for God's grace and mercy.

Thankful prayer remembers. Thankful prayer puts into perspective. This kind of prayer asks God regarding our needs because it acknowledges needs already met. We are alert in prayer because we remember prayers already answered. Every prayer should include a thankful attitude.

Plunging deeper into faith always involves a deepening commitment to prayer. Prayer is always at the center—at the heart—of our discipleship and spiritual development. The closer our relationship with God grows, the more we want to talk with Him in prayer.

So, in prayer, we remember that God is great and He is good and so we thank Him for our food—and for every blessing He has provided.

Day Twenty-Five: Saying Grace

Points to Ponder

Verse to Remember: Colossians 4:2: "Devote yourselves to prayer; stay alert in it with thanksgiving."

Questions to Consider: Am I consistently devoted to spending time in prayer? How might I be more alert in my prayers? Why do I think praying with thanksgiving is so important?

Today's Bible Reading: Proverbs 28–29.

Declaring Internationally

Declare His glory among the nations,
His wonderful works among all peoples.

1 Chronicles 16:24

Blessings are not given only to people like you.

No greater blessing is given to us than the gospel message. This is our hope and our life. Christ died for our sins, which separated us from Him. He paid the price for our sins, and through His sacrificial death we can be forgiven and made new. He rose from the dead, conquering sin and death and hell. By repenting of our sins and believing on the Lord Jesus, we can be saved.

The gospel is our greatest blessing. Through Christ we can have life: eternal and abundant. Our sins are totally forgiven, our hope is fully secured, and our salvation is completely accomplished. This is truly good news.

But blessings are not given to hoard. The Lord does not give us the message of the gospel to keep to ourselves. He hasn't blessed us so we can stockpile our blessings. He has blessed us to bless and He has given us the message of salvation to share.

~~~~~

Our blessings are not to hoard; they are to declare.

~~~~~

We are to "declare His glory" to the nations. We tell the nations of the message of God's love and redemptive plan. We tell "His wonderful works" to all people everywhere.

I spent two weeks with a young man in a West African country. He was a relatively new believer who felt called by God to be a pastor and to preach the message of the gospel to his people. As far as we could tell, this young man was the first pastor in the history of his small people group. For two weeks I talked with him morning and night about the message of the Bible and his responsibilities as a follower of the Lord Jesus.

This young man drank in everything he could. He read his Bible faithfully and peppered me with questions all day long. He was like a sponge with water, soaking up everything he could learn.

The blessings Christians take for granted in America were not taken for granted in this West African nation. Our church buildings are comfortable. The church in this young man's village met under a tree. Do you know what they did when it rained? They got wet. I did not tell him that in our country believers are prone to skip church if it's raining because they might get damp on their walk between their car and the church building.

We have water fountains in our church buildings and give out water bottles to those unwilling to stoop. This village had only a deep well that had been dug through the kind action of mission volunteers from the United States. The women carried water in jugs on their heads back to their huts. There were no water fountains in the church buildings they didn't have.

In church services in our country, we have the Bible on our phones or carry one of our many copies of the Bible with us when we attend worship services. There, Bibles are a precious and rare commodity. Church members share their Bibles with each other. There is no easy access to study Bibles or commentaries or Christian books.

I was reminded that I have been blessed to grow up in my country where I can hear the message of the gospel easily and attend church conveniently. But that blessing is not just for me to have. I am blessed to bless. And I have the privilege of declaring God's glory and work among all nations and all peoples—even among people who are different than I am.

Through our prayers and financial support, we can bless missionaries and ministries around the world. Through our mission trips and support, we can be directly involved in taking the message of the gospel to peoples faraway. And, of course, all of us can take the message of the gospel to those in our communities and schools and workplaces and regions.

We are blessed by God so that we will be a blessing. And, to the glory of God, we can be a blessing near and far. We can be a blessing to our neighbors and classmates and to people who live on the other side of the world.

I have been blessed and so I am to bless. I have heard and experienced the wonderful message of God's love and salvation, so I am to tell others of that blessing.

Our blessings are not to horde; they are to declare. The blessing of the gospel is not only for us and those who look like us or live near us. This blessing of the gospel is for all people. And so we declare God's glory and wonderful works to all nations and all peoples in all places at all times.

〜〜

DAY TWENTY-SIX: DECLARING INTERNATIONALLY

POINTS TO PONDER

Verse to Remember: 1 Chronicles 16:24: "Declare His glory among the nations, His wonderful works among all peoples."

Questions to Consider: Have I seen my blessings as an opportunity to bless others? Is there a way for me to declare God's glory and works to the nations? Am I actively supporting missions personally? Is there something more I could do?

Today's Bible Reading: Proverbs 30–31.

The Responsibility of the Blessed

Much will be required of everyone who has been
given much. And even more will be expected of the one
who has been entrusted with more.

LUKE 12:48

Have you been given much?

You might tend to think this focal verse applies to someone else. It must apply to someone more talented than you. Perhaps it is only for those with more education or greater skills or more resources. But might it apply in some way to you?

You have been blessed in many ways. You have ready access to food and education and transportation and opportunity. Many parts of the world have little accessibility to those things. Counting your blessings this week might well have reminded you of the abundance you enjoy. It might have reminded you that you are one of the "everyone" who has been given much. You might be "the one" who has been entrusted with more.

Those blessings are more than just material blessings. Every opportunity to worship the Lord in a church service and every chance to attend a Bible study group is a blessing. Access to Christian radio stations and to Christian books are blessings. You have great spiritual blessings given to you by the Lord.

So, what are you to do with those blessings? What is the responsibility of the blessed?

According to God's Word, much is required and expected of you. Your blessings have been entrusted to you as a gift—but not just for you to enjoy. You are required to use those blessings in a way that will bless. You are expected to bless others through those blessings given to you.

And, the more you are blessed, the greater God's expectations for you. The more blessings you receive, the more the Lord expects from you.

DOUG MUNTON

—∞∞—

The more you are blessed, the greater
God's expectations for you.

—∞∞—

Perhaps you've seen the incredibly gifted athlete who was lazy. He or she never trained very hard, never practiced with any vigor, and didn't hustle much in games. Or perhaps you know bright, intelligent students who never did homework and settled for academic mediocrity. Maybe you know talented musicians or artists who never honed their skills. These people have been given much, but they never meet the expectations.

What about the one who has trusted Christ as Savior and has experienced the blessings of faith but never does much with those blessings? The Lord has blessed you so you will do something great with those blessings. He has expectations of you. He wants you to hone the skills He has given you so that you will use those skills to be a blessing. He desires that you learn the truths of His Word so that you will use that knowledge to be a blessing.

Responsibility comes with your blessings. Expectations come with your talents and skills and resources and opportunities. The greater the blessing, the greater the expectation.

I want you to apply this focal verse in three areas: your talents, your treasure, and your time. Each of these is a blessing God gives you that you can use to bless others.

Bless others with your talents. Perhaps you are a gifted teacher or musician or singer. You can use that talent to honor the Lord and to bless others. You can teach children or teenagers in your church. You might sing in a choir or play in an orchestra. If you have a talent in sports, you might coach a kids' league. If your talent is driving nails, you can build homes for the needy or do repairs for the elderly.

Bless others with your treasure. As God blesses you financially, you can support the ministry of your church. You can participate in missions through your giving. Someone out of work can be blessed by your "no strings attached" gift. You might help an elderly person on a fixed income or a young family that is stretched thin at Christmastime.

Bless others with your time. Time is an opportunity. You can use it to do good for others. Rake some leaves, shovel some snow, or volunteer at church. Older people can invest in the lives of the younger. Younger folks can visit a nursing home. Give a listening ear and a sympathetic hearing. Help with a school play or with clean up after an event.

You have been blessed, haven't you? See those blessings as reasons to bless others. Be responsible. Use your talents, treasure, and time to bless others as you have been blessed.

The Lord expects something from you.

∽∾∾

Day Twenty-Seven: The Responsibility of the Blessed

POINTS TO PONDER

Verse to Remember: Luke 12:48: "Much will be required of everyone who has been given much. And even more will be expected of the one who has been entrusted with more."

Questions to Consider: Am I using my talents, my treasure, and my time to bless others? Are there specific ways I can begin to use the blessings I have received to bless someone else?

Today's Bible Reading: Acts 1–2.

Day Twenty-Eight
Saved to Bless

For we are His creation—created in Christ Jesus
for good works, which God prepared ahead of time
so that we should walk in them.

EPHESIANS 2:10

Salvation is about more than a ticket to heaven.

Heaven is awesome. That last sentence is a terrible understatement, isn't it? Saying that heaven is awesome is certainly not enough to describe the greatness and the wonder and the excitement of heaven. Saying heaven is awesome is like saying the sun is bright: true, but inadequate.

Heaven will be a place of joy and discovery, absent of problems and turmoil. My reading of Scripture convinces me that heaven will be fun and adventurous and whatever words are better than "awesome." But salvation is about more than heaven.

When we are saved, we are "created in Christ Jesus." That means that we are made new by Him. Our sins are forgiven and our lives are changed. We are born again. There is a spiritual rebirth. We die to the old life and live new lives in Christ. We are God's creation physically in that He made us. We also become God's creation spiritually when He saves us.

We are not saved *by* good works. The two previous verses—Ephesians 2:8–9—tell us that we are saved by grace through faith and not by our good actions. We place our faith in the good work done for us by Christ on the cross and not in our own goodness. But, we are saved *for* good works. There is a purpose to our salvation that involves our good actions and right conduct in this life.

A clear purpose to our salvation is that God wants us to do good works. God wants us to be a blessing to our world through the good works that we perform. Our lives are to become example and blessings to others. Our behavior is changed by our salvation.

Think of this purpose of salvation for a moment. Have you considered this fully yet? Let's imagine a conversation.

If I ask, "For what purpose did God save you?" You might say, "He saved me so that my sins would be forgiven completely and I will go to heaven one day."

"That is right. For what other purpose?" "Well—" you stammer, surprised there is something else. "I suppose He saved me so that I will worship Him and give glory to Him."

"Very true. For what other purpose has He saved you?" "Hmmm," you say, buying time as you struggle to think of any other reason for this great gift from God, "Well, I guess He might have saved me so that I will do something good while I'm still here on earth. I suppose, now that I think about it a bit, God has saved me so that I will make some sort of impact on this world by how I live and what I do here."

Exactly. God saves you, not only so you will be forgiven and can enjoy the wonders of heaven one day and not only so you can enjoy the closeness of genuine worship and intimacy with Him. He also saves you for the purpose of empowering you to do the good works He has for you to do. He has blessed you so that your life will be a blessing to this world.

Our focal verse reminds us that God has prepared these good works for you to do ahead of time. That is, before you were saved—even before the world was created—God had a purpose for your life and salvation. He had good works planned for your life. He gave you the abilities and gifts and opportunities you would need to do the good works He already planned for you to do.

God blessed you with the gift of salvation so that your life will be a blessing to this world. Your life is to be a means by which others see the light of truth and the power of faith. Your life is to be an example. Your lifestyle is to be a model. Your service and ministry is to be a blessing.

God wants you to be a blessing to the world through
the good works you perform.

Salvation is not just about what you get. You do get forgiveness and heaven and hope and a host of other wonderful blessings in salvation. It is about more than that. Your Savior saves you to give as well as to get. He has good works, acts of kindness, thoughtful deeds, and important service planned for your life. He saved you for more than heaven alone. He saved you for good works which He planned for you long ago.

God saved you to bless.

—〰〰—

Day Twenty-Eight: Saved to Bless

Verse to Remember: Ephesians 2:10: "For we are His creation—created in Christ Jesus for good works, which God prepared ahead of time so that we should walk in them."

Questions to Consider: What are some of the good works God saved me to do? Is my life a blessing to others? Is my lifestyle reflecting the Lord and His goodness? Is there some good work that God wants me to do today?

Today's Bible Reading: Acts 3–4.

Chapter Five
COME ON IN: CHOOSING A MISSIONAL LIFE

Those plunging deeper into faith realize that they are invited by God to join Him in His work in this world. God's purpose is for more than just ourselves; we are to influence others. We have a mission from God to impact our world for His glory.

On a Mission

For the Son of Man has come to seek and to save the lost.

LUKE 19:10

"Zacchaeus was a wee little man; a wee little man was he."

You have to have grown up in church and be old enough to know the song referenced in the first line. It was a children's song for Sunday school and Vacation Bible School and such events. As a child I sang that song with gusto. It was a favorite of mine. There was something about the picture of short, little Zacchaeus climbing a sycamore tree to see Jesus that triggered my imagination. But this is more than a story about a short tree-climber. It is about a Man on a mission.

The story of Jesus and Zacchaeus is recorded in the nineteenth chapter of the book of Luke. Jesus was passing through the town of Jericho where a rich, yet vertically-challenged tax collector lived. Zacchaeus was too short to see over the shoulders of the crowd that lined the road where Jesus walked. So, he ran up ahead as fast as his little legs could take him and climbed a tree in order to catch a glimpse of the famous Teacher strolling through town.

Then, the strangest thing happened. Jesus walked right up to the tree where Zacchaeus had perched and told him to hurry up and come down because He had to stay at Zacchaeus' house that very day.

What a shock that must have been. Jesus called him by name (how did He know?), told him to hustle down, and invited Himself over to stay at his house. I'll bet Zacchaeus didn't see that coming.

The Bible tells us that Zacchaeus came down quickly and welcomed Jesus joyfully. To imagine that Jesus cared for him was spectacular in the extreme. But this was not a popular move with all the folks in Jericho. People began to complain, "He's gone to lodge with a sinful man!" (v. 7). Of all the prominent citizens Jesus could have dined with that day, Zacchaeus was a terrible choice as far as the people of Jericho were concerned. He was a tax collector, a traitor, and a cheat.

DOUG MUNTON

Tax collectors have never been popular, I suppose. Who really enjoys paying taxes? But Zacchaeus was not just collecting taxes; he was collecting taxes for a foreign government. Roman rule was unpopular with the Jewish citizens and paying taxes to them was even more detested. Add that to a system that was rife with corruption and bribery and theft and one has the making of great discord.

Zacchaeus was lumped into that big category of "sinners." We are all sinners, of course. But we tend to categorize some into the more scandalous types. And tax collectors were certainly in that camp as far as the people of Jericho were concerned.

The time spent with Jesus, however, changed the diminutive tax collector. He gave evidence of repentance and a changed heart when he said, "Look, I'll give half of my possessions to the poor, Lord! And if I have extorted anything from anyone, I'll pay back four times as much!" (v. 8).

These were astonishing words. A man who seemed willing to betray his own country for money was now willing to give away half of all he owned to the poor. A man who made a living by extortion and bribery now was going to make that right with those he had wronged. These were not the ordinary actions of the ordinary tax collector. Something had changed within.

Jesus responded by saying, "Today salvation has come to this house, because he too is a son of Abraham" (v. 9). He noted the changed priorities in Zacchaeus' life and his new faith. This faith was the same faith displayed by Abraham long before.

In our focal verse, we see Jesus' commitment to the mission of seeking the lost. His mission is saving lost souls. There is a suggestion that we ought not to be surprised to find Jesus staying in the home of sinners or talking to the wayward. He is on a mission, after all, to seek them and to save them.

≈≈≈

People matter to the Lord.

≈≈≈

IMMERSED

This is a mission worth noting. Jesus cares about people who are messed-up, doing wrong, and spiritually confused. He loves people who seem unlovable and cares about those who seem beyond hopeless. People matter to the Lord.

The mission of Jesus—and, therefore, the mission of His disciples—is about more than helping nice people be nicer. It is about helping dead people find life. It is about helping messed-up people find healing. It is about helping lost people find salvation.

Jesus spent His time here on a mission and sets the example for us to follow. His model of compassion for lost people is to be our model. His example of caring for people is for us to follow. His recognition that people need saving faith more than money or position or power applies to us as well. We are to join Him on this mission to show people the message of the gospel.

Even wee little men in sycamore trees.

〜〜〜

DAY TWENTY-NINE: ON A MISSION

POINTS TO PONDER

Verse to Remember: Luke 19:10: "For the Son of Man has come to seek and to save the lost."

Questions to Consider: What do I find most surprising about the story of Zacchaeus? How can I join Jesus on His mission to seek and save the lost? Who do I know that needs to hear the message of God's grace?

Today's Bible Reading: Acts 5–6.

It Just Takes One

There is joy in the presence of God's angels over
one sinner who repents.

LUKE 15:10

Just one salvation is all it takes to bring joy to heaven.

Some think of people like pennies——there are lots of them and they aren't worth much individually. God thinks of them like diamonds—each is unique and of tremendous value.

Our focal verse nestles in the middle of three parables told by Jesus. The first tells of a lost sheep, the second of a lost coin, and the third of a lost son. Each tells the same message. There is great rejoicing over the return of the lost.

While I don't fully understand why, the Lord loves to see even one lost man or woman or boy or girl repent of their sins and trust Him as Savior. He values them so much that He rejoices over their redemption. He is like a shepherd diligently seeking a lost sheep and rejoicing over its discovery. He is like a widow desperately sweeping for a lost coin and overjoyed at its uncovering. He is like a father looking to the horizon for a prodigal son and throwing a great celebration at his return.

God rejoices over the repentance of just one. That is the idea of our focal verse. God rejoices in the presence of the angels in heaven that one is saved. That is how valuable just one life is to the Lord. That is how valuable one life should be to us.

We see this more clearly when we personalize it. We might think of the salvation of one little boy as no big deal. But it is a big deal if it is our son or grandchild. The salvation of *that* little boy, of course, matters greatly to us. When the person is personal to us, we can see the value more clearly.

There was a poor little farm boy who grew up in a home where he never heard the message of the gospel. But, for some reason, there was a powerful interest deep within him to know the truth. He described it as wanting to become a Christian, though he was unsure what being a Christian fully meant.

⸺⸺⸺

God rejoices over the repentance of just one.

⸺⸺⸺

One day at school, he spoke with a playmate about his desire to become a Christian. The friend was unable to tell him how to become a Christian, but he did invite him to a special event at his church where they would tell little boys and others how to be saved. The little boy loved the idea and eagerly rushed home to see if his father would take him to church that night.

Joy turned to disappointment for the little boy. His father didn't want to go, but blamed it on the old car that could not be driven until it got an overdue oil change. The little boy volunteered to do it himself. The father amazingly agreed. Who sends their young son out to change oil in a car? The son made a mistake and drained the transmission fluid instead of the oil. No one would be driving the car that evening.

The little boy was crushed. He felt as though he might never get another opportunity to hear the message he so desperately needed. Even his father was saddened to see his son so disappointed.

Some months later, the little boy was at school when his young friend told him about another special event at his church where he could learn about becoming a Christian. The little boy was thrilled to hear the news and rushed home to ask his father to take him.

This time, the father went with his son to church. They heard the message of God's redemptive work and how sinners can repent of their sins and be saved because Christ died on the cross and rose from the dead. That night the little boy repented and believed on the Lord Jesus. He was saved. He became a genuine Christian. And, to his delight, his father made the same commitment the very next night. It was a dramatic change in that family.

I am so happy for the decision of that little boy. You might not care too much about one little boy being saved. But that little boy grew up to become my father. His life matters to me, and I rejoice in the story of his salvation.

When I am tempted to stop caring about whether people come to know Christ or whether our church reaches anymore people, I remember that little farm boy and how important he is to me and to God. I can remember how one lost sheep matters to the shepherd and one lost coin matters to the widow and one lost son matters to the father.

I need to remember how one lost person matters to the Lord. I need to remind myself of the joy the angels witness in heaven when just one sinner repents. I need to picture the rejoicing and thrill of heaven.

It just takes one.

⎯⎯ᴧᴧᴧ⎯⎯

Day Thirty: It Just Takes One

Verse to Remember: Luke 15:10: "There is joy in the presence of God's angels over one sinner who repents."

Questions to Consider: Have I considered lately how much one sinner matters to God? How does this verse change my perspective about sharing the gospel? Is there someone I know who is lost that I can pray for and look for opportunities to share my faith with?

Today's Bible Reading: Acts 7–8.

Day Thirty-One
Representing the King

We are ambassadors for Christ; certain
that God is appealing through us, we plead on
Christ's behalf, "Be reconciled to God."

2 Corinthians 5:20

What a great job this must be.

Countries send ambassadors all over the world. They serve as representatives of their home country. They build relationships, discuss the policies of their country, and seek to influence their hosts in ways that are beneficial to their homeland. While this job could be challenging, even dangerous, it must be very fulfilling. Ambassadors are at the cutting edge of the foreign policy of their government.

One important part of plunging deeper into faith is to recognize and activate your role as an ambassador for Christ. You, if you know Christ as your Savior, are a representative of the King. You are His ambassador wherever you go—at your home, at your job, or in your school. And this is a great job.

Some of Christ's ambassadors are called to serve in faraway places such as those who serve as career missionaries in distant countries. Others serve as His representatives closer to home. They are ambassadors at their construction site or in their college dorm. But all of those who know Christ are called to represent Christ in this world.

The focal passage lays out the job description for our role as ambassadors for Christ. We plead with others to be reconciled to God. We do this because we know that God is doing the pleading through us. We are participating in God's work of reconciliation.

God doesn't call us to be ambassadors because He needs us or is somehow dependent on us. He could certainly do all He does without any help from us. If He wanted to, God could form the clouds into the plan of salvation. He, being God, could move the stars so they form words that tell people of their need to be reconciled to Him. God doesn't need us; he wants us.

We have the opportunity and privilege of participating in God's work. God wants to use us to share the message with others. He has chosen to use His disciples as the means by which others hear the good news. We become ambassadors. We represent Christ in our world.

⸻

We have the opportunity and privilege
of participating in God's work.

⸻

As ambassadors, we are not to adopt a "take it or leave it; it's all the same to me" mentality. We "plead on Christ's behalf." The missional life is a life of great passion for evangelism. This life cares deeply about others coming to know Christ as Savior and Lord. "Pleading" is a strong term. It carries the idea of deep conviction and passionate concern.

If you've been to a sporting event, you have seen passion. Fans cheer on their team and bemoan every failure. They care deeply about the outcome and want desperately to see their team succeed. Nowhere is this more evident than watching parents and grandparents at children's sporting events. They plead with their kids to perform adequately so the family name is not besmirched. They delight in their victories and revel in successes.

Ambassadors for Christ are not disinterested observers. We are deeply invested in the desire to see others find salvation. We know that Christ is the only hope for forgiveness of sins and eternal life. Our witness is filled with passion for people to respond to the message. We are thrilled when one repents and responds to the gospel.

The message of ambassadors for Christ is, "Be reconciled to God." Men and women are separated from God by sin. God made us for fellowship with Him, but our sins have broken that fellowship and estranged us from the Lord. Reconciliation is the act of restoring that fellowship and relationship with God. We can be reconciled because Christ, on the cross, paid the debt we owed. We can be reconciled because Christ died so that we can live. In salvation, we can be brought into right relationship with the God who created us.

The missional life is the recognition that we join God in His work of reconciliation. We can't save anyone, of course. Only Christ can do that. But we can plead with people to trust the finished work of Christ on the cross. We can urge people to turn from sin and find forgiveness in Jesus.

You are not the king. There is only one God, one Savior, and one King. But you can join with other disciples in serving the King as an ambassador. You can allow the Lord to appeal to others through you. You can urge those around you to respond to the message of the gospel. God can use you as a means of accomplishing His work in this world.

You represent the King in your home, neighborhood, school, and workplace. You are an ambassador, busy with this important work of calling people to follow the King. It is a great job.

—∿∿—

Day Thirty-One: Representing the King

Verse to Remember: 2 Corinthians 5:20: "We are ambassadors for Christ; certain that God is appealing through us, we plead on Christ's behalf, 'Be reconciled to God.'"

Questions to Consider: In what ways can I be an ambassador for Christ? Where does God want me to be an ambassador? Why am I to plead with others?

Today's Bible Reading: Acts 9–10.

When Beggars Find Bread

Then they said to each other, "We're not doing what is right.
Today is a day of good news.
If we are silent and wait until morning light, we
will be punished. Let's go tell the king's household."

2 Kings 7:9

"Evangelism…is one beggar telling another beggar where to get food."[2]
If you were a poor, starving beggar who stumbled upon a vast supply of
delicious, fresh bread, would you tell everyone or keep it to yourself?

Long ago, the king of Aram besieged the city of Samaria. The city
was surrounded by thick walls, so a frontal assault was suicidal. Instead,
the king decided to lay siege to the city. He surrounded the city, kept
produce and sustenance from being brought in, and steadily starved the
city into submission.

Slowly but surely the citizens of Samaria began to starve. Prices for
what little food remained skyrocketed. Some even resorted to cannibal-
ism. The situation seemed hopeless in the extreme.

In the face of utter despair, the Lord spoke to the people of Samaria
through His prophet Elisha. He announced to them that the very next
day, food would be so abundant they would buy six quarts of fine meal
or twelve quarts of barley for just one small silver coin. That seemed
impossible. One official said that couldn't happen even if the Lord
opened windows in heaven and poured down grain.

Near the gates of the besieged city where they begged for food were
four men with skin diseases. They could not enter the city because of
their condition and they couldn't leave the city because of the Aramean
army. But desperate times call for desperate measures. Reasoning that
they would soon starve if they stayed where they were, they decided to
go to the Aramean camp. If they were killed, they were killed.

[2] D.T. Niles, *That They May Have Life* (New York: Harper & Brothers Publishers, 1951),
p. 96.

To their shock, the four beggars found the camp empty. The Lord had sent the sound of a vast army to the ears of the Aramean soldiers and they fled for their lives, leaving all their food and belongings behind. Before the amazed eyes of the starving beggars was a vast storehouse of food, livestock, clothing, and gold.

They stuffed food into their mouths until their sunken cheeks bulged. They gathered and hid loot as quickly as they could dig holes. And then, they began to think about all those starving people back in Samaria.

"Are all these blessings just for us? Don't others need these same blessings? Shouldn't we tell other beggars about this bread?"

What would you do under similar conditions? Would you keep the food and wealth for yourself, or would you share this good news with others?

Salvation is a gift God has given to beggars like us. We don't deserve it and we didn't earn it. God blessed us with the Bread of Life and we can eat of this bountiful harvest of forgiveness and hope and eternal life. But what about the rest of the world? Is this gift of salvation just for us, or is it to be shared with the rest who are facing spiritual starvation?

The four beggars came to believe that their actions were wrong. It was not right for them to enjoy the blessing themselves without thought for those who were starving. This was a day of good news, and good news is not something we keep to ourselves. Good news is for sharing. Bread is for starving beggars. They decided to go tell others.

I'm sometimes satisfied to keep the good news to myself. After all, I have found the blessing of salvation and I want to enjoy it. So, I eat all the spiritual food I can stuff down and bury the treasures of faith in the sand. But I'm not doing what is right. I remember all those starving beggars who don't know about this bounty. I remember that they are hungry and needy—just as I was. And I am reminded that good news is for sharing, not for burying.

Good news is for sharing, not for burying.

If you know Christ as your Savior, that is good news. You have found the Bread of Life and it is bountiful. But it isn't just for you and it isn't right to keep it for yourself. Good news is for sharing. There are other beggars who need this same food you have discovered.

Let's go tell.

Day Thirty-Two: When Beggars Find Bread

Verse to Remember: 2 Kings 7:9: "Then they said to each other, 'We're not doing what is right. Today is a day of good news. If we are silent and wait until morning light, we will be punished. Let's go tell the king's household.'"

Questions to Consider: In what ways am I like the four beggars in this story? Is it right for disciples to keep the good news of God's salvation to themselves? Who do I know that needs this good news?

Today's Bible Reading: Acts 11–12.

DAY THIRTY-THREE

Everywhere We Go

Those who were scattered went on their way proclaiming
the message of good news.

ACTS 8:4

It was a really tough day.

First, Stephen was stoned to death, becoming the first martyr of the church. Then, Acts 8:1 tells us, "On that day a severe persecution broke out against the church in Jerusalem." The followers of Christ, many of them brand-new believers, were scattered all over the region by this wave of persecution.

The murder of Stephen was a disconcerting event for the early church. Stephen was a good and godly man. He is described in Acts 6:5 as a man "full of faith and the Holy Spirit." When deacons were selected to serve the needs of the church, Stephen's was the first name mentioned. He was full of grace and power. Stephen was the all too rare combination of a kind, compassionate servant and a bold witness. His death must have carried equal portions of sorrow and fear for the Christian community.

The persecution didn't end with Stephen on that difficult day. Emboldened by the death of Stephen, Saul and others began a systematic approach to what they hoped would be the eradication of the fledgling church. Saul entered home after home of believers and dragged men and women off to prison. The persecution became severe for believers all over Jerusalem.

While the apostles stayed in Jerusalem, most Christians left the city for the relative safety of other towns and villages. But they did not leave the message of the gospel behind. The focal passage tells us that they proclaimed the saving message of the gospel everywhere they went.

These young believers could leave their homes behind, but not their faith. They took their faith—and shared it—everywhere they went.

Two very interesting things resulted from the scattering of the church

DOUG MUNTON

154

all over the region. First, the gospel was quickly spread and second, a seed was planted in the heart of a persecutor.

The gospel was truly spread through the persecution of the early church. Many were forced to leave their homes in Jerusalem behind, but they were able to bring something far more valuable with them. They took the message of the gospel to every community they entered. More disciples were made and more churches were birthed in cities and towns far and wide.

━━∿∿∿━━

The liberating gospel goes everywhere we go.

━━∿∿∿━━

Some even took the message of salvation to the gentiles in Antioch. The good news spread like windblown wildfire among these Gentile hearers, and large numbers gave their lives to Christ. Philip, another godly deacon, shared the good news with a government official from Ethiopia and the gospel came to Africa. The message that had been restricted to the smaller region of Jerusalem now spread far beyond the borders of Judea.

A second result of the persecution was the example that was given to one of the most zealous of all the persecutors. Saul was a committed Pharisee who felt he was doing God a favor by trying to stamp out the church. He watched as Stephen died with forgiveness on his lips. He saw the courage of these Christians in the face of imprisonment. He observed the power of the gospel in the face of persecution. The more he stomped, the more the gospel flames spread.

Soon, Saul encountered the truth of the gospel and gave his life to Christ as Savior and Lord. He later became a great intellectual force for the faith and was used to author, under the supernatural guidance of the Holy Spirit, many books in the New Testament. He was used to spread the gospel far beyond the region as he became an apostle to the Gentiles. The example he saw in these early believers became the model he followed the rest of his ministry.

We are to take Jesus everywhere we go. Problems can't crush the truth, and persecution can't imprison the message. The liberating gospel goes wherever we go. The message goes with us to our jobs and to our neighborhoods. The message goes with us to our colleges and on our business trips. Everywhere we go, we take the message of the living Lord who can forgive sins and give eternal life.

Even persecution could not kill the gospel. They might have been able to take Stephen's earthly life, but not his eternal one. They might have been able to persecute the church, but not to conquer it.

Take with you the gospel message on every trip and to every job. Look for opportunities to share the message through every victory and every difficulty. Be on mission for the Lord. Even on the hard days.

〜〜〜

DAY THIRTY-THREE: EVERYWHERE WE GO

Verse to Remember: Acts 8:4: "Those who were scattered went on their way proclaiming the message of good news."

Questions to Consider: What stands out to me about the faith of these early Christians? In what tangible ways can God use me to share the faith with others?

Today's Bible Reading: Acts 13–14.

I Can't, But He Can

Now go! I will help you speak and I will teach you what to say.

EXODUS 4:12

There are a thousand reasons why you can't be a witness for the Lord and a thousand more why you can't serve in some ministry responsibility. You don't know enough. You are too reserved. You get nervous in serious conversations. Your life is imperfect. You sweat a lot. The sun is in your eyes. I get it. Sharing your faith with others is hard. Serving in ministry is difficult. You can't do it.

There is a myth that God uses only perfect people. Since when? He doesn't have any perfect people to use. God doesn't call you to be a witness or to serve Him in ministry because He thinks you're perfect. He knows your imperfections and weaknesses perfectly well.

We may be tempted to think God is dependent on some superstar getting saved. He desperately needs some political leader or rock legend to profess faith in Him to make it. God is not dependent on anyone. He doesn't need a superstar or you or me. He is fully capable of doing His work without any of us. But He wants us to join Him in His work. He wants imperfect, excuse-laden people like us to participate in His mission. He calls us to do so.

Moses was not exactly jumping at the chance to obey God and lead the people of Israel out of bondage in Egypt. Instead of responding to God in faith and confidence, he expressed doubt and gave excuses. When God called him to lead, Moses responded with whining.

The Lord told Moses to go because He was sending him to Pharaoh to lead the Israelites out of Egypt. Moses responded in Exodus 3:11 with the less than courageous words, "Who am I that I should go?" Those words are not confidence personified.

The Lord told Moses to go and that He would be with him every step of the way. Moses responded in Exodus 3:13 with the less than inspiring reply: "If I go." He wasn't really one to jump into a commitment, I guess.

⸻∿∿⸻

God isn't waiting for you to be perfect or powerful.

⸻∿∿⸻

After Moses complained to God that the Israelites might not believe him, God showed him the miraculous sign of the staff that became a snake and then the snake that became a staff. He then had Moses put his hand in his cloak and it became leprous; when he inserted it again, it was healed. How did Moses respond? Another excuse.

"Please, Lord, I have never been eloquent...I am slow and hesitant in speech" (Exodus 4:10). Moses told the Lord he couldn't obey because he wasn't such a great speaker. He tried an after-dinner speech once and it didn't go so well. He messed up the words and developed a stuttering problem. There was no hope for any improvement. This just could not work out.

The Lord is very aware of our limitations and our weaknesses. He certainly knew about the speaking difficulty of Moses. But He reminded Moses that He made his tongue and He called him anyway. God knows your limitations and He chooses to use you anyway.

The focal verse is God's promise to use us despite our weaknesses. It is God's reminder that He empowers weak and imperfect people to accomplish His purposes. He is able to overcome our deficiencies and to accomplish His work through us whatever those weaknesses may be. He may even use our weaknesses as a means of reminding us of our dependence on His power and not our own.

Interestingly, despite all God's assurances, Moses still didn't want to obey. He responded to God with the words, "Please, Lord, send someone else" (Exodus 4:13).

I wonder if you have ever talked like that to God. Perhaps God has impressed on you that you needed to give a verbal witness of faith to a friend and you said, "Please, Lord, send someone else." God convicted you to use your time and talents to teach a small group in your church or to serve in some ministry area and you said, "Lord, I think you have the wrong person. Please find someone else." God invited you to join Him in His work and you said, "I think you have the wrong person."

Here is the good news. God does not expect you to do this mission alone or in your own strength. He is fully aware of your inabilities and weaknesses and promises His presence and His power. He will empower your witness. He will enable your ministry service. He will help you to speak and He will teach you what to say.

He isn't waiting for you to be perfect or powerful. He's waiting for you to recognize His ability to use you despite your inadequacies. He waits for you to see His great strength and to depend on Him and not yourself. He wants you to trust Him to do great things through you.

You can't do it, but He can.

—⁓⁓⁓—

Points to Ponder

Verse to Remember: Exodus 4:12: "Now go! I will help you speak and I will teach you what to say."

Questions to Consider: Why do I think Moses responded to God as he did? What excuses have I given to God for why I can't do what He wants me to do?

Today's Bible Reading: Acts 15–16.

The Kind of Person God Uses

This saying is trustworthy and deserving of full acceptance:
"Christ Jesus came into the world to save sinners"—and
I am the worst of them.

1 TIMOTHY 1:15

"You can't even join until you admit you aren't worthy!"

I often say that to people at our church. We are a church that is filled with imperfect people who are unworthy to be a part of God's family. In fact, every church is made up of people like that. We are all fallen people who have gotten mercy instead of what we deserve. We receive God's unmerited love instead of the judgment rightly due us.

We don't have our act together. We tend to carry around a lot of baggage. We have fallen flat on our faces more than once. Our church, like every church, has people who have messed up in many ways. And yet, God wants to use disheveled people like us.

The enemy promotes what I call "The Big Myth." The Big Myth says that God can't use someone like me because of all the sin of my past. I've messed up too many times to ever be able to serve the Lord in any meaningful capacity. My sins are beyond forgiveness.

I've got good news. God is able to forgive fully by the blood of Jesus shed on Calvary. And, He is able to use sinners, even the worst of them, to join Him in His work in this world.

Paul was an amazing servant of God. He preached fearlessly, started churches all over the place, and was a preeminent theologian. But his was not a perfect past.

You may know that Paul once persecuted the church. He consented to the killing of Stephen. He personally terrorized Christians and threw many into prison. He fought against the very truth of the gospel, and he fought against the Lord Himself. These are some of the reasons why Paul labeled himself "the worst of sinners." His was certainly not a perfect past.

DOUG MUNTON

God wants to use you to accomplish His purposes in this world. He wants to use you, not because you are perfect or because He is dependent on you, but because He loves you and wants you to experience the joy of service. He wants to use you even though He knows your past problems. He wants to use you, knowing the idiosyncrasies and quirks of your personality.

⚍⚍⚍

God wants to use disheveled people like us.

⚍⚍⚍

One of the reasons Paul was used so greatly by God was because Paul was fully aware of his unworthiness to be used so greatly by God. His recognition of the depth of God's grace led to a depth in his service and his ministry.

My story of conversion does not sound as dramatic as some. I came to know Christ as my Savior while still relatively young. I did not have to go through the terrible struggles some faced. I avoided addictions and gang warfare and never involved myself in assassination plots.

But my need for grace and forgiveness was just as real as the most notorious sinner. My need for God's mercy was just as deep as that of anyone. I sinned against a holy God and my sin separated me from God and heaven as widely as anyone's sin ever did. Nothing in me deserves the privilege of forgiveness or grace. And nothing in me makes me worthy of being used by God. But God has used me just as He wants to use you. Our roles may be different; our pasts may be different; our abilities may be different. But God has the same power to use you or me or anyone else willing to surrender to His lordship.

God wants to use you. Let that sink in for a moment. God wants to use you. He wants to make a difference in this world through your life. He wants your life to be a trophy of His grace and your ministry to make an impact in this world.

God does His extraordinary work through ordinary people just like you. Ordinary people can be forgiven by God's extraordinary salvation.

Ordinary people can overcome all their past and all their problems and all their weaknesses by the extraordinary working of God in their lives.

God isn't looking for perfect people. He is looking for willing people. He is looking for sinners who have discovered His salvation. He is looking for the weak who are willing to trust Him for their strength. He is looking for those willing to follow Him wherever He leads.

God wants to use you. Are you willing?

—∽∧∿—

Day Thirty-Five: The Kind of Person God Uses

Verse to Remember: 1 Timothy 1:15: "This saying is trustworthy and deserving of full acceptance: 'Christ Jesus came into the world to save sinners'—and I am the worst of them."

Questions to Consider: Is God really able to use me? Am I willing to surrender fully to the Lordship of Christ and allow Him to use me to accomplish His purposes?

Today's Bible Reading: Acts 17–18.

Chapter Six

DEEP WATER: LIVING OUT YOUR FAITH IN THE REAL WORLD

When we plunge deeper into faith, we realize that our faith is not private, nor only about heaven. We live in a world that needs the hope of the gospel, and we are to live out our faith in tangible ways. Living out our faith in a needy, confused and fallen world is deep water that needs to be navigated for God's glory.

They Are Like Christ

> For a whole year they met with the church and taught
> large numbers, and the disciples were first called
> Christians in Antioch.
>
> Acts 11:26

"You people act like Christ!"

The term "Christian" has lost much of its meaning in our culture. People call themselves Christian based on heritage or background or because they aren't something else. It doesn't necessarily mean that the person has trusted Christ as Savior or that they are committed to plunging deeper into faith.

There was a time, however, when the word "Christian" meant something more than heritage. It was originally given to the believers in Antioch because they sounded and acted like Jesus Christ. It was so clear that they were following the teaching and example of Jesus that it seemed natural for them to be identified by the term.

Why were believers first given this title in Antioch? It seems that designation had something to do with the quality of the discipleship of these followers of the Lord. Serious disciples look like Christ.

Some of the believers who were scattered as a result of the persecution of Stephen ended up in Antioch. This was a Gentile area and they began to share the message of the gospel with their new neighbors. Many of them turned to the Lord. The church in Jerusalem heard the news and decided to send one of their most trusted members, a man named Barnabas, to check on things.

Barnabas arrived in Antioch to find numerous followers of the Lord. He was delighted and he began to encourage them in their faith. Barnabas was good at that. Almost every time we read of Barnabas in the New Testament he was involved in encouragement.

He did two specific things in regard to the church at Antioch. First, he encouraged deepened discipleship. His encouragement specifically was "to remain true to the Lord with a firm resolve of the heart" (Acts 11:23). In other words, Barnabas did all he could to strengthen their understanding of, and commitment to, the Lord. He urged them to obey the Lord and to allow Him to change their inward heart, not just their outward behavior.

⌁⌁⌁

Serious disciples look like Christ.

⌁⌁⌁

Discipleship always involves outward obedience and inward resolve. God changes our behavior on the outside and our motives on the inside. When the inward heart is changed, the outward actions are changed. Acting like Christ goes to the very core of our being.

The second thing Barnabas did was to enlist the help of Saul—better known to us as the apostle Paul. Saul was relatively new to faith himself, but he was growing and learning about the Lord's purpose and plan every day. Antioch was to be his very first ministry experience. Barnabas and Saul formed a powerful team.

The Bible tells us that Barnabas and Saul taught the church in Antioch for a whole year. They taught large numbers of new believers who were anxious to learn and to live out their faith. The church was growing numerically as new believers joined, and the church was growing spiritually as the believers met for intense discipleship and training.

Note that the disciples were not called Christians until they had learned and studied for an entire year. Deep discipleship does not happen in a moment; it takes the seasoning of time.

Mushrooms grow overnight, but oak trees take decades.

Nothing can take the place of consistency in our spiritual development. For some of you, this is the first consistent devotional period in your Christian life. I hope it will not be the last. It is my prayer and hope that these 40 days will encourage you toward a lifetime of knowing and following the Lord. Discipleship involves following the Lord day after day and week after week throughout the lifetime God gives you. Nothing can replace consistency in your walk with the Lord.

As a result of the discipleship of the believers in Antioch, there was a noticeable change in the way they acted and thought. People around town noticed the difference. Classmates and neighbors observed new attitudes and priorities. Something was different. They were acting, thinking, and talking just like their Savior, Jesus Christ. So, someone called them "Christians." The name stuck.

Nothing can be a better designation for us. Discipleship is about following Christ, and when we do it correctly, people are able to see Christ in us. They are able to see that Christ is the one who has changed our actions and our attitudes. Christ is the motivation for our living and for our service. He is the model for our behavior and our spirit. We are at our best when identified as Christians.

I urge you to follow the example of these early Christians. Get connected with other believers in a church. Learn all the Lord has for you in His Word. Deepen the commitment of your inward heart as well as your outward actions. Put into practice the faith each day. Show Christ to others through your lifestyle and your attitudes. Let others see Christ in you. And they just might say, "You act just like Christ!"

Day Thirty-Six: They Are Like Christ

Verse to Remember: Acts 11:26: "For a whole year they met with the church and taught large numbers, and the disciples were first called Christians in Antioch."

Questions to Consider: Am I connected with other people who are helping me grow in faith? Am I helping anyone else grow in faith? Are those around me able to see Christ in my lifestyle and attitudes?

Today's Bible Reading: Acts 19–20.

Living with Integrity

They could find no charge or corruption, for he was trustworthy,
and no negligence or corruption was found in him.

DANIEL 6:4

What charge might be found if one dug deeply enough into your life?

Integrity, or the lack thereof, is one of the leading indicators of whether or not you are successfully living out your faith in the real world. What you do and don't do, how you live and don't live, are of vital importance to your witness and your influence.

Daniel had an amazing life. He lived out his faith in a foreign land where they worshipped foreign gods. He was successful in a culture that didn't know the Lord and didn't reward faith. He stood out among others because he lived out the principles of God's Word and practiced them whether popular or not.

The sixth chapter of Daniel tells how Darius, the mighty king of Babylon, made Daniel one of his top three administrators. This was quite exceptional for an outsider like Daniel. He stood out in his ability and in his dependability. He was so outstanding that Darius decided to make him the top man among all his satraps and administrators. The king saw an extraordinary spirit in Daniel. We know this spirit came out of Daniel's deep immersion in his faith.

With political success came political intrigue. The other satraps and administrators were jealous of Daniel's power and began to look for a charge to bring against him. They reasoned that they might gain power if Daniel lost it. So, the search began. What charge might they find if they dug deeply enough?

To their disappointment, the politicians could not find any charge or corruption. Daniel could not be bribed, seduced, or coerced. He was not the normal sort of leader. At least, he wasn't the sort of leader they were.

Three characteristics stand out about Daniel. First, he was the same in public and in private. His rivals looked far and wide but could find no corruption. They found no skeletons in his closets and no hypocrisy in his private life. Integrity may be described as who you are when no one is looking. Daniel was trustworthy in public because he was trustworthy in private.

∽∿∾

Your lasting influence and witness in this world
will be determined by your integrity.

∽∿∾

A second characteristic of Daniel was that he worked hard and honorably. His enemies found no negligence or corruption. Daniel must not have shirked his duties or failed to do assigned work. He had a strong work ethic, which is lacking in much of our modern world. It wasn't just that he worked hard, he also worked honorably. There was no corruption, no bribes under the table, no shady deals.

A third characteristic of Daniel is his consistency in faith. He was strong as he stood before the king because he was strong as he knelt before the King of Kings. His faith was not an occasional fix but a constant foundation.

This consistency showed itself soon enough. The enemies goaded Darius into signing an irrevocable law that no one could pray to anyone but the king for 30 days. But Daniel knew God's Word about praying only to the Lord. The Bible tells us that when Daniel heard about the decree, he knelt in prayer three times a day to pray to his God "just as he had done before" (Daniel 6:10).

His enemies had him. They reported him to the king. Darius, to his dismay, was forced to follow his own law and to throw Daniel in the lions' den. God, however, rescued Daniel from the lions and he was restored to his position and the name of the Lord was exalted in Babylon.

We love this story and the example set by Daniel. But there is a question that should arise. What if that had been you or me? If they were digging through our trash and looking through our computers and sifting through our lives, would they find this kind of integrity?

In many ways, our lasting influence and witness in this world will be determined by the integrity of our hearts. In the long run, who we are is more important than our talents or abilities or charisma. How we live is more important than what we say.

Integrity gets to the heart of living out our faith in the real world. Taking the plunge of discipleship means we determine to follow the Lord publicly and privately. It means we live by His standards and follow His teachings—whether those things are popular or not. It means our work, our studies, our leisure activities, and our private moments all fall under the lordship of our great King.

Integrity means we live our life as though our greatest enemies could discover all the details. Even if no one else ever knows our secrets and never searches for our weakest points, we are to live with integrity. Even if we are not rescued from the lions' den or given a position of influence, we are to live with integrity. Even if we never see the results of our influence, we are to live with integrity. Because integrity is not just what we do, it is who we are. Even when no one is looking.

~~~~~

DAY THIRTY-SEVEN: LIVING WITH INTEGRITY

POINTS TO PONDER

Verse to Remember: Daniel 6:4: "They could find no charge or corruption, for he was trustworthy, and no negligence or corruption was found in him."

Questions to Consider: What would I not want others to find out about me? Am I consistent in my faith? Where does my private life not match the perception others have of me?

Today's Bible Reading: Acts 21–22.

Live Worthy

> Just one thing: live your life in a manner worthy
> of the gospel of Christ.
>
> PHILIPPIANS 1:27

Few verses are as clarifying and prioritizing as this.

These words in Philippians focus our attention on what really matters if we are to live out our faith in the real world. They cut through the static and get to the heart of the matter. We discover a straightforward priority. We are given a clear focus.

We can never, of course, be worthy of the gospel of Christ. The whole point of the gospel is that we are unworthy and must believe on the One who is. We could never be worthy of the sacrifice Jesus made for us. Never are we in any way worthy of His suffering or His salvation. Only He is worthy. But we can live worthily. Our priority is to live "in a manner worthy of the gospel of Christ"—in a way that brings honor to Him.

We can be never be worthy *of* salvation but we can live worthily *in* salvation. Salvation has ramifications beyond the glory of eternal life in heaven. It also changes the way we live our lives in the real world of the here and now. There are five specific applications I want us to make as we consider how we can live worthy of the gospel.

The first area of applying the concept of living worthy of the gospel has to do with our behavior. If we are to live out the emphasis of this verse, our behavior is an excellent place to start.

Recognizing the price of sin as shown in the cross, our behavior should reflect the holiness of God. Salvation is freedom from sin rather than a license to sin. The gospel points out the terrible consequences sin carries. The sacrifice of the cross is a reminder of the ugliness of sin and the death in which it results. Living worthy of the cross remembers that lesson and lives out that message through a desire to avoid sin and live in holiness.

DOUG MUNTON

The second application of living worthy of the gospel concerns our attitude. This verse affects our attitude as well as our actions. The gospel is a clear reminder of the love of God. We can see His grace and mercy personified. The humility of Jesus on the cross is the attitude we are to emulate.

⟶∼∧∼⟵

We can never be worth *of* salvation, but
we can live worthily *in* salvation.

⟶∼∧∼⟵

Our lives are not merely the sum of our actions. Actions are seldom divorced from attitudes in God's Word. Often, our attitude is the primary factor in the behaviors we choose. Living out the gospel means we choose to have the same attitudes that we see in the Redeemer.

A third area of application of the focal verse's call to live worthy of the gospel involves our gratitude. Living worthy of the gospel carries with it the idea of appreciating what Christ has done for us. Our lives are changed in response to the salvation He provided for us.

The good news is not something to be ignored. It is cause for a thankful spirit and a grateful heart. Reflecting on the greatness of God's grace is enough to lead us to a life of thanksgiving and appreciation. The deeper our understanding of the gospel, the deeper our thankfulness for Christ's work will be. In some sense, we will live worthy of the gospel only as well as we are grateful for the gospel.

A fourth area of application of the biblical mandate to live our lives worthy of the gospel concerns our mission. We live worthy of the gospel through understanding the mission the gospel gives us.

The gospel carries responsibilities. We are to grow as a disciple and make the gospel known to others. The gospel message leads to our obedience to serve the Lord and share the Lord with others who also need that message. We join the Lord in His mission of making disciples of all nations.

A fifth application to make concerning the idea of living worthy of the gospel involves our motivation. Salvation is not about us. We didn't earn it and we don't get the credit for it. It is about the loving Savior who gave Himself for us.

In a similar way, our lives are not about us. Living worthy of the gospel includes our recognition that the motivating factor for our lives is not our glory, but His. His glory becomes the motivation for our lives when we live worthy of the gospel.

Let this verse ruminate in your mind and heart. Allow the gospel of Christ to change you at every level. You can never *be* worthy but you can *live* worthy. This is the focus and priority of a life that plunges deeper into faith.

Day Thirty-Eight: Live Worthy

Points to Ponder

Verse to Remember: Philippians 1:27: "Just this one thing: live your life in a manner worthy of the gospel of Christ."

Questions to Consider: What might change in my life if I live this verse out fully in my life? Why do I think it matters that I live my life in a manner worthy of the gospel of Christ?

Today's Bible Reading: Acts 23–24.

Faith Works

> But someone will say, "You have faith, and I have works."
> Show me your faith without works and I will
> show you faith from my works.
>
> JAMES 2:18

Peanut butter and chocolate go together.

I love peanut butter and I love chocolate and the love is doubled when the two are combined. I love candy bars that combine the two ingredients. Ice cream with both ingredients has become a favorite. For me, these two flavors just taste great together. They are a natural mix.

Faith and works go together, and that combination is not subject to the whims of taste buds. God Himself has combined these two ingredients as necessary parts of tasty theology.

The book of Hebrews talks in great detail about the importance of faith. The very next book in the New Testament is the book of James. That book speaks in great detail about the importance of works. Are the two books at odds? Of course not. Faith and works go together in the life of a believer.

A great way to think of this connection is like this. Salvation is activated by faith and authenticated by works.

When we say salvation is activated by faith, we are saying that works cannot save us. We cannot do enough good things to change the sin of our past. We trust what Jesus has done for us, not what we can do for ourselves. In salvation, we place our faith in Christ and not in works.

You will never be able to work your way to heaven. Only by placing your faith in the finished work of Jesus can you be saved. His death, burial, and resurrection are the means of salvation. Faith in Christ Jesus activates salvation.

When we say salvation is authenticated by works, we are acknowledging that the Lord of salvation changes our lives. When we are saved, we become new people with new hearts. Our actions, attitudes, and ambitions are changed. Our works are the means by which we show our faith. They become evidence of a transformed life.

⚬⚬⚬⚬⚬

Salvation is activated by faith and authenticated by works.

⚬⚬⚬⚬⚬

Saying some words you don't mean won't save you, of course. Some have made empty commitments without any genuine salvation. Genuine faith always leads to genuine changes. If there are no good works, there are reasons to question the veracity of a person's faith. The doubt as to the truthfulness of that faith can be raised. Salvation is authenticated by works.

True faith, therefore, always leads to good works. The two cannot be fully separated. Today's focal verse declares, "I will show you faith from my works." My works are the evidence of my faith.

When I was a teenager, a speaker talked to our church group one evening. He asked us to imagine that we were on trial for being Christians. In this imaginary scenario, it had become illegal to be a follower of Christ and we stood accused. He asked us to imagine we were at a jury trial for the crime of being a Christian. A jury listened to the evidence based on the actions of our lives.

One lawyer called witnesses who spoke to the evidence that we were Christians. They might say things like, "This young man is always going to church. He must be a Christian." Or, "This girl reads her Bible and is thoughtful and kind, so she must be a Christian." The other lawyer called witnesses to condemn us. These witnesses gave evidence that we weren't really Christians after all. They said things like, "This guy uses the same language we use. He tells the same dirty jokes. He can't be a Christian." Or, "This girl has a terrible temper and gossips all the time. She can't be a Christian."

Then the speaker asked a question that caused me to think long and hard. He asked, "If you were on trial for being a Christian, would there be enough evidence to convict you?" Okay, maybe it isn't the most profound idea ever, but this event really made me consider the relationship of my faith to my actions and attitudes.

The speaker suggested the same thing the book of James suggests. Those who are saved through faith ought to evidence their faith through works. The two concepts are intrinsically linked. Our good works come from our faith. Our faith leads to our good works. The two are connected. It is unnatural, spiritually speaking, to have one without the other.

The outworking of our faith and works is an important part of living out faith in the real world. Genuine faith leads to changed lives. Changed lives lead to a powerful witness in the world.

Faith and works go together like peanut butter and chocolate. Is anyone else hungry?

Points to Ponder

Verse to Remember: James 2:18: "But someone will say, 'You have faith and I have works.' Show me your faith without works, and I will show you faith from my works."

Questions to Consider: In what ways are faith and works connected? In a trial, would there be enough evidence, based on my lifestyle, to convict me of being a Christian?

Today's Bible Reading: Acts 25–26.

Day Forty
Faith That Blesses

Seeing their faith, Jesus told the paralytic,
"Son, your sins are forgiven."

Mark 2:5

What kind of person tears a hole in another man's roof?

The story recorded in Mark 2 is amazing. Jesus was in the city of Capernaum and a huge crowd of people came to see and hear Him. Some were curious and some were skeptical, but the swarm of people around the house grew so large that they couldn't all fit inside. They spilled out the doorway and massed around the perimeter of the house as Jesus spoke.

Worming their way through the crowd that day were four men carrying the stretcher of a paralyzed friend. They'd heard reports of the miraculous ability of Jesus and wanted to bring their paralytic friend to experience His touch. But there was a problem.

The crowd pressed so thickly that they couldn't get through. People who had arrived earlier were unwilling to move and, try as they might, the men could not get their needy friend to Jesus.

What more could be done? They tried and were unsuccessful. They couldn't get through. Oh well. But that is not how the story ends. The Bible tells us they climbed up onto the rooftop and began to tear a hole in the roof above where Jesus was so they could lower their friend down to Him.

I love their tenacity. I love their innovation. I love their willingness to go the extra mile and to sacrifice and sweat and work.

Can you imagine what it must have been like for the crowd inside? They were listening politely to Jesus when they heard people walking on the roof. As Jesus continued to speak, they noticed strange scratching sounds. Then, pieces of the ceiling began to fall on them. Suddenly sunlight came pouring in through a small hole in the ceiling—a hole that grew larger and larger. They saw men tear open the ceiling until it was quite a large hole—large enough to lower a man through. "What kind

DOUG MUNTON

184

of men do this?" they must have wondered.

The Bible tells us they lowered their paralyzed friend down from the rooftop right in front of Jesus. As the crowd watched in amazement and brushed ceiling debris and dust off their tunics, Jesus spoke. "Son, your sins are forgiven."

Jesus dealt with the biggest problem the paralytic faced. His biggest problem was not the inability to walk. His biggest problem was the sin that separated him from God and His holiness. After forgiveness was granted, Jesus dealt with the man's secondary need for physical healing.

The man was healed and forgiven and gave glory to God. The crowd was startled and amazed and learned how important a matter salvation is. The town must have talked about this event for years. It was replayed around dinner tables and campfires again and again. One part of the story, however, is often overlooked.

Our focal verse points out a part of the story we often fail to recognize. The Bible says, "Seeing their faith, Jesus told the paralytic, 'Son, your sins are forgiven.'"

Notice whose faith motivates Jesus' words. It isn't the faith of the paralytic. The Bible says, "Seeing their faith." The faith of the friends is the catalyst for Jesus' words of forgiveness.

Here is the principle we must not miss: If we are faithful, God will bless others through our faith. When we live by faith, God blesses others through the faith He sees in us. God could do it without us, of course. Jesus certainly could have come to the paralytic's home had He so desired. He did not require the faith of the friends to bring healing. But the faith of the friends was the catalyst for the miracle Jesus chose to perform in the life of this sinful and paralyzed man.

⁓⁓⁓

If we are faithful, God will bless others through our faith.

⁓⁓⁓

If you will live a life of faith and discipleship, God will bless others through your life. He will use you as a means by which others find forgiveness of sin and hope for eternity. He will use you as a means by which people hear the message of the gospel. He will use you to help others grow in their faith. Your example, your willingness, and your sacrifice will be used by the Lord to bless others. The faith the Lord sees in you will be used to bless others.

Live by faith. Trust God to do great things through you. Be bold and innovative. Go the extra mile. Tear a hole in a roof for the benefit of man and the glory of God. And let God use you to make a difference in this world and in eternity.

DAY FORTY: FAITH THAT BLESSES

Verse to Remember: Mark 2:5: "Seeing their faith, Jesus told the paralytic, 'Son, your sins are forgiven.'"

Questions to Consider: Why do I think these friends were willing to go to such lengths to help their friend find Jesus? Might Jesus bless others through my faith? Are there some great things God wants to accomplish through my faith?

Today's Bible Reading: Acts 27–28.

Conclusion

The 40-day journey has ended, but plunging deeper into faith never ends this side of eternity. You have begun some healthy practices during this 40-day emphasis that can become healthy habits for the rest of your life. Let me suggest where you can go from here.

First, continue the regular practice of spending some time each day reading the Bible and praying. If you have followed the daily Bible reading in *Immersed*, you have read the books of Proverbs, John, and Acts. Continue reading each day, working through the rest of the New Testament and the entire Bible. I've made it my practice to read the entire Bible at least once each year and I commend that approach to you. Read the word and spend time in prayer each day just as you have for the past 40 days.

Second, be active in a local church and in a small group Bible study. The church is imperfect because it is filled with imperfect people like you! Still, God made the church for us. He wants us to be actively involved with other believers and to sharpen each other through our fellowship. Find a Bible-teaching church and get plugged in.

Third, begin to apply your faith in your everyday life. Use your talents, resources, and time in ways that honor the Lord. Look for opportunities to share your faith with others. Get involved with mission trips and mission support. Volunteer to teach at your church or to help in some form of ministry. Apply the lessons God teaches in His Word.

God made you and saved you for great things. Ask God to use you in doing great things for His glory!

Acknowledgments

Seldom has a pastor enjoyed the love, encouragement, and support of a church as I have with the wonderful people of First Baptist Church of O'Fallon, Illinois. It has been my great privilege to be their pastor for many years and I love this church dearly. The great members and the fabulous staff make the joys of ministry greater and the burdens lighter. I cannot thank them enough for the privilege of being a part of their lives, and I pray that the best is yet to be.

My family is great. They have sped the process along by their encouragement and slowed it down by being so much fun to be around. I'm thankful for both. They have proofread and suggested improvements and supported in every way. Vickie, my wife, has done so much work in making this book a reality. I've loved our years together and growing in my discipleship at her side all these years.